The Howse whi

Discovering Campden House and Gardens

Researched and written by

Mary Fielding

Mary Gray

Helen Kirkup

Edited by

Vanessa Rigg

Published by Chipping Campden History Society
The Old Police Station, High Street, Chipping Campden. GL55 6JW

Front & back cover illustration: The Hughes Bird's-Eye c.1750 by William Hughes. British Library. Inset: Detail of Sir Baptist Hicks attrib. Paul van Somer. By kind permission of the Trustees of the Middlesex Guildhall Art Collection

Photographs on pages 30, 37, 38, 42, 44, 46, 52, 53, 57, 61 and 82: Keyna Doran

Illustrations on title page, page 84 and diagram of aerial photograph within the inside back covers: Tom Ford

Graphic design: Keith Phelpstead

ISBN-10 0-9550866-5-5

FSC
www.fsc.org
MIX
Paper from
responsible sources
FSC® C004309

Printed on paper from sustainable sources

Vale Press

Printed and bound in Great Britain
by Vale Press Ltd, Willersey

Contents

Campden House Project

Chipping Campden History Society has been developing the Campden House Project for four years to record and disseminate the history of this important house and gardens, aided by grants notably from the Heritage Lottery Fund.

The project has involved a range of activities: archaeological surveys and excavations, archive and internet research, learning workshops, visits to places of interest, displays and events to inform the public, schools and local groups.

Many members of the Society and other volunteers have contributed to this project:

Frank Badger	Rowland Evans	Carol Jackson
Sue Badger	Debbie Ewing	Vin Kelly
Alan Barclay	Christopher Fance	Christina Kingsmill
Dale Boswell	Mary Fielding	Jane Kirby
Darrell Bowden	Diane Fine	Helen Kirkup
Jennifer Bruce	Margaret Fisher	Ken MacDonald
Michelle Burke	David Gabb	Pearl Mitchell
Sally Campbell	Alison Gough	Robert Montgomery
Jane Chapman	Mary Gray	Stephen Nixon
Amanda Collicutt	Jacob Greenslade	Trevor Parsons
Beatrice Corry	Robert Grove	Christina Reast
Alice Crummack	Eric Harding	Vanessa Rigg
Tim Crummack	Ann Hettich	Geraldine Rogers
Judith Ellis	David Hewitt	Annie Rolfe
Margaret Elsy	Dudley Holmes	Jill Wilson
Diana Evans	Nick Holt	Ros Young

Project Co-ordinator: Judith Ellis

Foreword

This book marks the successful completion of a programme of research designed and run by Chipping Campden History Society into Campden House and its owner. Over a period of four years the insight gained has enhanced the knowledge and the appreciation of a site of architectural and historical significance.

While professional assistance was obtained in certain instances, the vast majority of the work was done by volunteers. Their commitment and loyalty to the project was constant, best illustrated by those who continued the archaeological dig in the worst of winter weather. Profound thanks go to all of the volunteers who contributed, and to those who do so much for the Society year upon year.

I wish to acknowledge with gratitude the cooperation of the Landmark Trust for granting access to the grounds, and to Chipping Campden Town Council for their support. Thanks also go to Martin Cook for overseeing the archaeological excavations, and Tony Roberts of Archeoscan for supervising the geophysical surveys. Both provided invaluable expertise.

Finally, a special thank you to the Heritage Lottery Fund whose generous grant made this research possible.

Robert Montgomery
Chairman

Chipping Campden History Society
Bringing local history to life

Introduction

What did Campden House and Gardens look like? That question has probably been asked by all who have seen the ruined site over the centuries. Visitors to Chipping Campden will have peered through the extraordinary Gatehouse standing by the church and wondered about the beautiful but curious buildings they could see. Campden House was a Jacobean masterpiece and its highly engineered grounds are a rare example of an English Renaissance garden. Built in the early 17th century for one of the richest men in England, the house stood for a mere three decades before it was burnt to the ground in 1645 during the Civil War. After the fire, the house was not rebuilt; orchards were planted on the magnificent terraced gardens and the surviving buildings were used as cowsheds and apple stores. Yet it is this neglect that has made the site so important today. Most if not all the gardens from this period have been lost, swept away with the changes in fashion. Because of its brief existence and subsequent neglect, this garden layout survives unaltered and its ancillary buildings still stand. As such, it is a Scheduled Monument, a site of national importance to Garden History, and it also contains some of the finest examples of Jacobean garden architecture in the country. Now in the ownership of the Landmark Trust, the future of the site and the protection of these unique gardens and buildings are secure.

Despite its national significance, there has been remarkably little research undertaken here. In the past, Paul Everson has written a paper on the gardens, there is a RCHME field survey and the University of Southampton conducted a small geophysical investigation. The most complete study is by the Landmark Trust's Historian, Caroline Stanford. New information came to light when their restorations were carried out and she has done invaluable work in ensuring that what little material survives is preserved. The lack of research is probably due to the shortage of available evidence; almost no documentary sources have been found relating to the construction or early years and there are no contemporary images.

Aware of the importance of the site but also of how little investigation has been conducted, Chipping Campden History Society initiated a research project. It began in 2014 with a geophysical survey funded by a grant from the Bristol and Gloucestershire Archeological Society. There followed archival research including the transcribing of 16th and 17th century manuscripts relating to Baptist Hicks, visits to and the study of houses and gardens of the period, and consultation with garden historians and other experts. Work culminated in three community excavations made possible with a grant from the Heritage Lottery Fund. This book is the result of those investigations. It does not tell the story of the site from its beginnings to the present day, instead it tries to recreate what it was like in its short-lived but glorious heyday whilst also shedding new light on the life and character of Baptist Hicks.

By gathering together all the available information for the first time, this is an attempt to answer that all important question:

What did Campden House and Gardens look like?

Ruins of Old Campden House, c.1900. Jesse Taylor.
By permission of Gloucestershire Archives and CCHS

Sir Baptist Hicks attrib. Paul van Somer. Believed to have been painted in 1618 when Hicks was 68, it now hangs in the Supreme Court, Westminster.
By kind permission of the Trustees of the Middlesex Guildhall Art Collection

"Ingenious Endeavours"

(Taken from the inscription on Hicks' tomb, St James' Church, Chipping Campden)

The Life of Baptist Hicks

Baptist Hicks was one of the many hundreds of men who made their money during the long successful reign of Elizabeth I and improved themselves even more when James VI of Scotland ascended the English throne as James I in 1603. Hicks was a mercer, supplying silks, velvets, cloth of silver and gold and other rich fabrics to wealthy merchants, members of the aristocracy and the Court; he also lent money at interest, becoming one of the wealthiest men in England. At the time of his death Hicks was worth £250,000 - £9.2 billion in modern terms.

At the Sign of the White Bear

Baptist Hicks' family had connections with Gloucestershire. His grandfather, John, was a clothmaker and owned fulling mills in Tortworth, near Berkeley and other property in Gloucestershire and Bristol. Robert Hicks (born c.1524), Baptist's father, left Gloucestershire and was apprenticed to a London Master ironmonger, Thomas Bartylmew. The Ironmongers' Company records a Robart Hycks registered as an apprentice in 1541 and Robard Hycks as a master in 1544 but at some point he began to trade as a mercer, based at the sign of the White Bear on the corner of Cheapside and Soper Lane (now Queen Street). He married Julian (a common female name then) Arthur of Clapton-in-Gordano, near Bristol, presumably around 1542 as his eldest son Michael was born in 1543.

Robert and Julian had six sons, three of whom – John, Francis and Hilary – died in infancy. The parish records of St Pancras, Soper Lane were lost in the Great Fire of London in 1666, and although there are records of his siblings, there is not one for Baptist. The surviving children were Michael, the eldest, Clement (or Francis Clement), and Baptist, born in late 1550/early 1551. Robert Hicks died in 1557 when Michael was 14 and Baptist was about 6.

It seems likely that the brothers all went to nearby St Paul's School for their early education. In due course Michael went up to Trinity College, Cambridge and then entered Lincoln's Inn. Whether Clement did the same is doubtful, but Baptist certainly did, matriculating from Trinity in 1568 and admitted to the Inner Temple in 1573. Entering the Inns of Court did not necessarily mean an intention to practice the law; at this period it was considered a kind of finishing school for gentlemen.

Map of the City of London showing the site of the Hicks' shop and other important sites and buildings, created from the Agas Map of c.1633, depicting the City of London in the 1560s. Annotated map courtesy of **The Map of Early Modern London,** *dir. Janelle Jenstad, University of Victoria. mapoflondon.uvic.ca. and London Metropolitan Archives, City of London Collage reference: 324941*

KEY

1. **St Paul's Cathedral**

2. **Guildhall** – *the centre of government for the City of London, where merchants held court, creating and revising the laws and regulations that established the city's wealth.*

3. **Mercers' Hall** – *The Mercers' Company is the foremost of the 12 principal Guilds of the City of London, based at Mercers' Hall. The Company acted as a trade association for exporters of wool and importers of velvet, silk and other luxurious fabrics.*

4. **The Great Conduit** – *A conduit brought clean piped water from the Tyburn to Cheapside, a facility which Hicks would introduce to parts of Campden.*

5. **Soper Lane** – *The Hicks' shop at the sign of the White Bear was at the top of Soper Lane, on the corner with Cheapside. At first the family lived over the shop, before moving to a house in nearby Milk Street.*

6. **St Peter's Hill** – *Julian Penne owned a house here where she lived, but also at times rented out.*

7. **Milk Street** – *Hicks lived in a house in Milk Street and died there in 1629.*

Little is known of Clement, except that he worked as a Searcher of Customs in Chester, a position which he may have gained through his brother Michael's influence. Letters from Clement to Michael in the Lansdowne Papers show that he was forever complaining of being short of money and despairing of his poor position.

Robert Hicks had left his family fairly well-off, but it was his widow who built up their real wealth. Julian Hicks re-married, probably in 1558 as soon as a decent interval had elapsed after the death of Robert Hicks. She became the wife of Anthony Penne, a friend of her late husband and it is as Mistress Penne that she is best known. She continued to run the mercer's shop at the White Bear, Soper Lane, and also had a lucrative business lending money. She must have been a formidable woman.

Michael Hicks had a large circle of friends, both from Trinity College and Lincoln's Inn, who were valuable contacts at Court. They may have introduced him to the service of William Cecil, Lord Burghley, in 1573 and in 1580 he became Burghley's patronage secretary, a very advantageous position, with plenty of scope for gifts from grateful – or expectant – petitioners. Michael's position as Secretary ended at Burghley's death in 1598, but he had become a close personal friend of his son Robert Cecil, who took over from his father and later became Earl of Salisbury. Between them, the brothers did very well out of Michael's connections and he was a very useful advocate on behalf of Baptist when debtors, including the King, were slow to repay loans.

Robert Cecil, 1st Earl of Salisbury (1563-1612) after John de Critz the elder
©National Trust Images
www.nationaltrust.org.uk

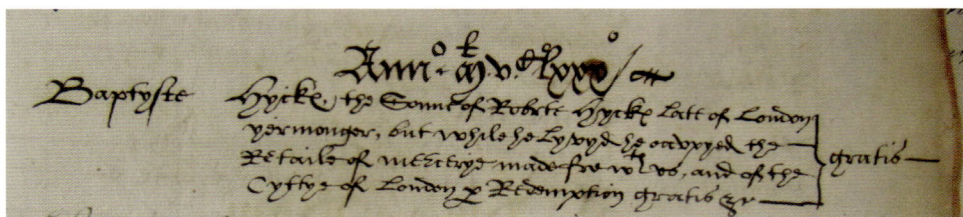

The entry of Baptist Hicks' Freedom from the Register of the Mercers' Company, Courtesy of the Mercers' Company. Hicks subsequently served three terms as Master of the Company, in 1603-04, 1610-11 & 1621-22.

The Rising Man

After his stint at the Inner Temple, Baptist was admitted to the Mercers' Company on 10th July 1577 'gratis' (i.e. with no fee payable) and presumably worked alongside his mother, learning from her experience in trade and business. She died in 1592 without leaving a will and Michael and Baptist drew up a legal Agreement regarding their mother's estate. Michael was established at Court, Clement was out of the way in Chester, and Baptist was running their mother's business, so it made sense for the eldest and youngest brothers to carve up the estate between them and pay Clement off with an annuity.

On 7th September 1584 Baptist Hicks married Elizabeth May, the eldest of thirteen children of Richard May, a Merchant Taylor. Baptist was 34 and she was about 22. They had five children between 1586 and 1694 – Juliana, Mary, Arthur, Elizabeth and Baptist – but only Juliana and Mary lived to adulthood. One of Elizabeth's sisters, Joan, married William Herrick, a royal goldsmith. Another sibling, Humphrey, born 1573, became what would be described now as a career politician, entering Parliament in 1605, rising to become Chancellor of the Duchy of Lancaster and a Privy Councillor – another important contact for Hicks.

Hicks was knighted on 24th July 1603, but this was hardly a significant honour, as anyone who had land to the value of £40 could receive a knighthood. James I, needing to raise money, had created hundreds of knights in his progress from Scotland to London. Between 23rd July and the King's coronation on 25th July some 427 men were knighted.

Sir Baptist and Lady Hicks were at pains to establish and maintain their rights of precedence and this caused a dispute with the Mayor and Aldermen of the City of London, who petitioned the King in 1607 complaining that *"some Knights Commoners, who still carried on trade in the City, claimed priority before some knighted later,*

Sir Baptist Hicks and Lady Elizabeth Hicks, both attrib. John Hoskins (c.1590-1665)
Private collection

and praying that the matter be referred to the Earl Marshal." Later historians writing in the 18th century refer to the role played by *"the junior ladies"* who *"took the lead so warmly in this important contest"* (Baldwin, 1773); *"Sir B. Hicks and his wife often bursteling about this Ceremony"* (Strype, 1720); and another unknown writer *"This tedious, troublesome, and chargeable contest was owing to the haughty deportments of Hicks and Herrick, and their imperious wives".* Four years later the matter had still not been resolved, for the City of London officials petitioned again for a decision and the Lords Commissioners finally decided in favour of the Aldermen.

From the Grant of Arms to Sir Michael and Sir Baptist Hicks, 1604. Leicestershire, Leicester & Rutland Record Office, courtesy of the Exton Estate. Baptist chose the motto 'Nondum Metam' meaning 'I have not yet reached my goal'. In this age of puns and double meanings, his "goal" could refer to heaven, but also allude to his worldly ambitions.

His trade and moneylending meant that Hicks was on business terms with a large number of people. Through his brother Michael he had contact with everyone at the Court and through the Mercers' Company, Goldsmiths' Company and others, he knew everyone worth knowing – and they knew him. Michael Hicks was a bon viveur, sociable and good company, who enjoyed hunting and had a passion for playing bowls. There is no sense from letters and other documents of Baptist being the same, but it would be good business practice to entertain and be entertained.

His status in the City led to him being nominated as an Alderman several times, but this was not an honour to be desired mainly because of the considerable cost of holding such an office. State and City of London papers are full of instances of men giving, possibly spurious, reasons why they could not take up office. Many men were prepared to pay a fine rather than accept the role. Baptist wrote to his brother:

"I have written these few lines to let you understand that very suddenly and very much unexpected there is a bill delivered up unto my Lord Mayor with the name of four commoners for the choice of an Alderman amongst which four I am nominated, and do very greatly fear that if speedily I make not the better Friend it will be my happ to be chosen and then will turne me to a farr greater trouble and suit than now it will do." (Lansdowne MS, British Library)

A letter to the Lord Mayor of London, written in 1604, shows that the King not only intervened in 1603 to prevent Hicks being elected as Alderman, but also ensured that he was excused duty as Sheriff the following year:

"Whereas in Dec. 1603 the king directed letters to the Lord Mayor requiring him not to nominate Sir Baptist Hicks to the place of an Alderman then being vacant and to take note that from thenceforth he should not be nominated if any like occasion should be offered. Now as the King understands that there will shortly be occasion for a sheriff to be elected for the city of London for the year ensuing he directs the Lord Mayor to cause the several companies on whom the election of a sheriff devolves, to forbear to elect the said Sir Baptist Hicks for the year ensuing as the king has graciously exempted him from the public services of the city in these cases."

"Baptiste Hickes" *signature on a letter to his brother* Lansdowne MS, British Library

"Silks, Satins, Velvets and Taffetas…"

Hicks was appointed Mercer to the Court of Elizabeth I in 1596, probably through the influence of his brother Michael, and State Papers have an entry on August 15th 1597 for providing cloth for a diplomatic mission:

"…Silks, Satins, Velvets and Taffetas, sold by Baptist Hicks, Merchant, to Sir Thomas Wilkes, on his going to Florence. Total £68 3s. 2d.".

By the time of the accession of James I, Hicks was already a wealthy man and in an excellent position not only to retain his position as Court Mercer, but also to lend considerable sums of money to the cash-strapped monarch and his down-at-heel courtiers. The Scottish Court was good business. He supplied *"velvets damasks and satins of the colour crimson"* for the Coronation in 1603, but these were still not paid for in 1606 and, he complains, the order was changed and he was left with 1,400 yards of cloth. He wrote to Michael, *"I find Scottish men are fair speakers and slow performers; being rid of them, I will cross them out of my books."* By 1607 the Crown alone owed him £24,000 of which £16,000 was for cloth and the rest *"advanced to meet the King's urgent occasions".*

He also had illustrious visitors to his shop in Cheapside. Sir Robert Cecil wrote to Michael Hicks:

"Sir W Rawley [Walter Raleigh] *and I dining together in London, we went to your brother's shop, where your brother desired me to write to my wife in anywise not to let anybody know that she paid under £3.10s a yard for her cloth of silver. I marvel that she is so simple as to tell anybody what she pays for everything."*

So Hicks was prepared to discount purchases by special customers to curry favour.

King James I in his Coronation robes by Paul van Somer, c.1620
Royal Collection

Sir Walter Raleigh attrib. William Segar, c.1598
National Gallery of Ireland

And on 20th April 1618 John Chamberlain wrote to Sir Dudley Carleton:

"The Chancellor [Francis Bacon] *was (at Mercers' Chapel) in as great pomp as when he went awhile ago to Sir Baptist Hicks' and Barnes's Shops to cheapen* [purchase] *and buy silks and velvets."*

Another notable customer was Elizabeth, Countess of Shrewsbury (Bess of Hardwick). The Shrewsbury Papers include a receipt *"of Robert Wilkinson on behalf of Sir Baptist Hicks for silver and gould stript stuffe"* and for brocade *"in flowers"* for the Countess of Shrewsbury, 25 June 1604.

Lady Frances Cavendish, Lady Maynard (1595-1613) attributed to Marcus Geeraerts, the younger
©National Trust Images
www.nationaltrust.org.uk

Frances was Bess's granddaughter. It is quite possible that this is the brocade *"in flowers"* mentioned in the receipt.

Portrait of a Lady of the Hampden Family, c.1610, artist unknown, wearing a dress embroidered with flowers
Photography by Erik Gould, courtesy of the Museum of Art, Rhode Island School of Design, Providence

Detail of skirt embroidered "in flowers" – another example of the luxurious cloth fashionable at the time

Naturally, family members received rich fabric from the accommodating Hicks, but did not always make best use of it:

"Sister Hicks, I did not know that the purple striped stuff with gold had been returned me again unless my brother had told me thereof and that you did not cut it to serve your turn for marring of the pattern. I pray you give me leave to tell you that no pattern comes amiss to me to pleasure you…"

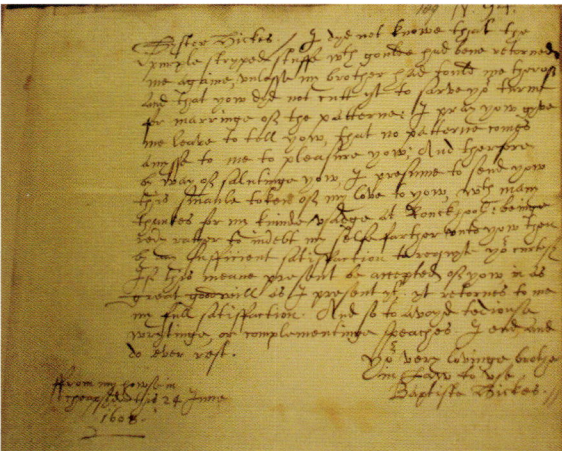

Manuscript letter from Hicks to his sister-in-law, Elizabeth, 1608
Lansdowne MS, British Library

Moneylender

Before the 16th century Canon Law forbade the lending of money at interest (usury) and it wasn't until the 1545 Act Against Usury that lending was permitted with a return of up to 10%. There were no banks or other financial institutions and so people were obliged to borrow from individuals against a bond to repay the loan at a specified time, which could be extended if the creditor agreed. Letters, legal documents and government records all testify to the large amounts of money owed to Hicks and by him and the difficulty he had in collecting repayment. He made full use of his brother's position; in 1611, for example, he wrote:

"Good brother, my occasions for monies … are many by reasone of my late purchased lands [probably Campden] for which as yet I am deeply engaged at interest… which hath incited me to caule for such monies as are due … my Lord Montgomery oweth me a very great sum … and my Lord of Pembrokke and others… whereof there hath not bene one penny payd … the other being for the payment of 1669 li 16 sh [due] in November last … for which somes I have often moved his honour to have satisfaction: and lately wrytt a letter to his Lordship importing my great occasions and how unwilling I was to attempt any commission that might be distasteful to his Lordshippe or my L. of Pembrooke, yet for all this I have received no payment…"

In another letter, of 1605, he asks Michael to remind the Lord Treasurer that he needs £16,000 of the King's debt to be repaid as *"I am shortly to marry both my daughters, to whom I am to give good rounde portions in marriage."* The *'good rounde portions'* were reputed to be £100,000 each.

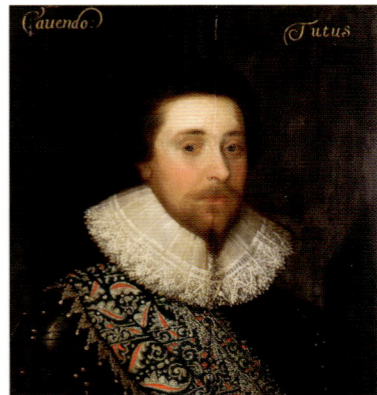

William Cavendish, 2nd Earl of Devonshire (1590-1628) by British (English) School.
©National Trust Images/Robert Thrift
www.nationaltrust.org.uk

Sometimes debtors fought back. Sir William Cavendish (1590-1628), grandson of Bess of Hardwick, was a profligate and extravagant young man who *"in his minority became indebted several times to Sir Baptist Hicks citizen and mercer of London in sums of money for wares and commodities…"*. By February 1614 Hicks and other creditors had waited several years for repayment and Cavendish was arrested and committed to prison. However, with or without the connivance of the Under Sheriffs of London, he escaped. He was then elected MP for Derbyshire in early 1614 and so became immune to arrest and imprisonment. Hicks believed that this was deliberate: *"that the said Sir*

William after his said arrest did use means to be elected knight of the said shire to the intent to free himself thereby of his said imprisonment". The creditors sued the Under-Sheriffs, but were then in turn accused of usury by Cavendish who, following the dissolution of Parliament in June, had escaped abroad.

A Man of Property

Apart from the lucrative sale of luxurious fabric and interest from lending money, Hicks acquired land and property throughout England either in lieu of unpaid debts or through direct purchase. This gave him an income from the rents. At the time of his death, he held 18 manors and significant holdings in Northumberland, Lincolnshire, Cheshire, Dorset, Leicestershire, Rutland, Kent, Essex, Gloucestershire, and, of course, London and Middlesex. He held a number of public and royal offices including Justice of the Peace for Middlesex, commissioner for oyer and terminer (i.e. an Assize judge), collector of Forced Loans and contractor for Crown lands. Most, if not all, of these and other offices provided opportunities for personal gain.

His interests were not just in England: he was an investor in the East India Company and in 1612 he was one of eleven men who purchased the Somer Islands (Bermudas), including their minerals and other resources, from The Company of Adventurers for £2,000. He had been an investor in the Virginia Company of London, but in 1624, after many tribulations, the Company was dissolved and taken over by the Crown. Hicks was appointed as a member of the Commission set up *"to examine the carriage of the whole business".*

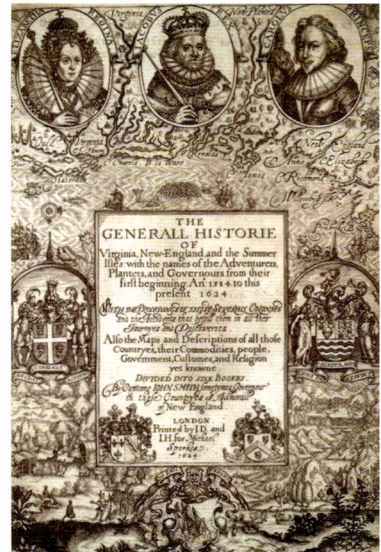

"The Generall Historie of Virginia, New-England, and the Summer Isles" by Captain John Smith, 1624

Living in London

Hicks continued to live at his house in Cheapside, even after the mansions in Kensington and Campden had been built. The shop remained at the sign of the White Bear, run by servants, then Hicks moved to Milk Street nearby, known for its rich merchants' houses. In December 1605 Baptist and Elizabeth's daughter,

Juliana, had married Edward Noel, not from her father's house in London, but from her uncle Michael's country house, Ruckholt, Essex. This seems to indicate that Baptist's residence in the City of London was not considered good enough for such an occasion. Judging by the detailed descriptions in her will, it is probable that, once it was completed, Lady Hicks spent much of her time at Campden House in Kensington.

Hick's Hall

In 1610 James I granted the Justices of the County of Middlesex *"a plot of land … to be for ever used and employed as a Sessions House, and for keeping a prison or House of Correction,"* and on this *"Sir Baptist Hicks built a very faire Sessions House of bricke and stone, with all offices thereunto belonging, at his own proper charges. On 13th of January 1612 … there assembled twenty-six Justices of the County, being the first day of their meeting in the place, where they were all feasted by Sir Baptist Hicks, and then they all with one consent gave it a proper name, and called it Hicks's Hall, after the name of the Founder, who then freely gave the same house to them and their successors for ever"* (Stow's Chronicle, 1633). Hicks Hall became known as a starting point for distances on the Great North Road (now the A1), and milestones were marked with the number of miles *"from Hicks' Hall,"* or *"from where Hicks' Hall formerly stood."* By 1777 Hicks' Hall was in very bad condition and was demolished. All that remains is a richly carved chimney-piece which was transferred to the new Sessions House.

From Ogilby & Morgan's map of London, 1676, showing 'Hix Hall', in **Ogilby and Morgan's Large Scale Map of the City As Rebuilt By 1676** British History Online

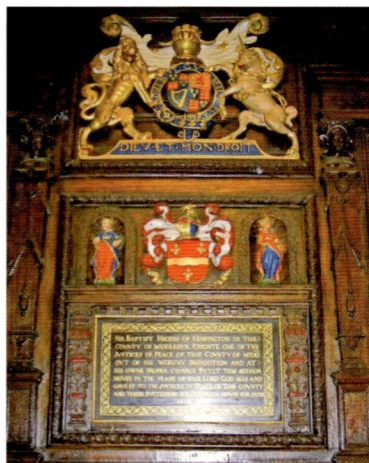

Overmantel of fireplace in Hicks Hall commemorating Hicks' gift, 1618

20

A year of change

1612 must have been a difficult year for Hicks; at the end of May, Robert Cecil died with Michael Hicks by his side. Then in August Michael himself died. The greatest shock – to the nation, if not personally– was the sudden death of Henry, Prince of Wales in November from typhoid fever.

The deaths of Cecil and Michael deprived Hicks of a source of support and assistance at Court. By 1612, however, he was in his early sixties and at the peak of his business life with many influential friends, business and Court contacts and so, apart from the personal loss of his brother, the impact on his business dealings was not as great as it might have been ten years earlier. Unfortunately, the death of Michael also meant the end of their correspondence, a valuable source of information.

The "Mannor of Campden"

Purchasing the Campden estate was to be a mixed blessing for Hicks. Anthony Smyth, the Lord of the Manor since 1593, had borrowed heavily against his land in Campden and several London men had their eyes on the prize. Hicks bought Smyth's debts and mortgages through agents and built up his acquisition of the manor, but he had a competitor, Lionel Cranfield. Like Hicks, he was a mercer, but he gained a position at Court and was a Member of Parliament in 1614 and 1621-22, when he was raised to the peerage as Earl of Middlesex. Cranfield wanted the estate as an investment and in 1609 commissioned reports which described the householders, their holdings and the rental values and provides us with important information about Campden.

Lionel Cranfield, 1st Earl of Middlesex (1573-1645), by Daniel Mytens the elder, early 1620s at Knole, Kent
©National Trust Images
www.nationaltrust.org.uk

Hicks probably took over the manor in 1609 or 1610 but Anthony Smyth died in 1611 and disputes and lawsuits ensued regarding ownership of the various messuages and repayment of loans. Cranfield believed that he had bought Campden Rectory, but Hicks thought it was included in his purchase from Smyth. Between 1610 and 1617 protracted legal proceedings took place, apparently resolved when Hicks purchased other property in Campden from Cranfield.

During this time there was also an ongoing dispute with the Smyth family. In 1616 Hicks finally petitioned the Lord Chancellor for a decision on his claim that the Smyths had refused to give him the deeds and other documents of the Manor and had retaken possession of some of the land and premises. In the same year Hicks brought a libel case against Augustine Jarrett, a Campden copyholder who had sided with the Smyths and allegedly abused Hicks in a letter. Finally in 1616 another claim was made against Hicks concerning the Campden estate, this time by Sir Paul Banning, whose father had lent money to Anthony Smyth. Banning maintained that the loan was still outstanding and claimed Campden Manor for himself. The case lasted until 1624 when the Court of Chancery finally found for Hicks.

Member of Parliament

Sir Baptist Hicks had a busy life, with the mercer's business, financial dealings, the many law suits, the building projects and acquisition of property, but in 1621, at the age of 71, he entered Parliament. The History of Parliament Online states that Hicks *"may at first have intended to stand for the junior seat at Tewkesbury, where his interest was already formidable, [he had been buying the former Abbey properties since 1612] but the 5th Lord Chandos wanted the place for a kinsman. Instead, he was found a seat at Tavistock, presumably through the mediation of Chandos, whose cousin had married Sir Francis Russell, the patron of that borough."* In 1620 Hicks had been created a baronet, an honour re-introduced by James I in 1611 to raise money, and in 1628 he was elevated still further by Charles I who created him Baron Ilmington and Viscount Campden.

Engraving of the House of Commons in 1624

He seems to have been active as an MP, serving on nine committees in his first term and making eight recorded speeches. He spoke from personal experience regarding a bill to protect creditors from abuses of bills of conformity. These bills allowed debtors to default on paying their creditors or repay reduced amounts and had been extensively issued by the Lord Chancellor, Francis Bacon. Hicks' one-time adversary, Sir Lionel Cranfield, led the charge against Bacon, believing the bills of conformity were harmful to trade. In this he was supported by his fellow merchants and moneylenders, including Hicks, who spoke in the debate which ultimately brought about the downfall of Bacon. *"One Dorrington owing him £200, being protected by the lord chancellor, is now fled, and so he hath lost his debt. ... Sir Henry Finch, Mr. John Finch and Mr. Nathaniel Finch, owing him likewise £200, have the like protection… and so he is also debarred to recover that debt also by any course of justice. ... Another, owing him £200 more, of which he had judgment against his debtor, yet delayed the execution of it... till at length he procured means from the lord chancellor to protect him…"* Hicks further declared that he was, *"as he rid* [rode] *in street in London, attached* [i.e. arrested] *for seeking duly his own."* (Proceedings of the Houses of Parliament 1621.) He remained MP for Tewkesbury until his elevation to the House of Lords in 1628.

Death

The Right Honourable Lord Hicks, 1st Viscount Campden, died in London on 18th October 1629 after a short illness, at the age of 78. He is, however, not buried in a London church close to his business interests, but in an imposing marble monument, possibly by Nicholas Stone, in St James' Church, Chipping Campden, which benefited substantially from his munificence. Hicks' chaplain, John Gaule, said at his funeral:

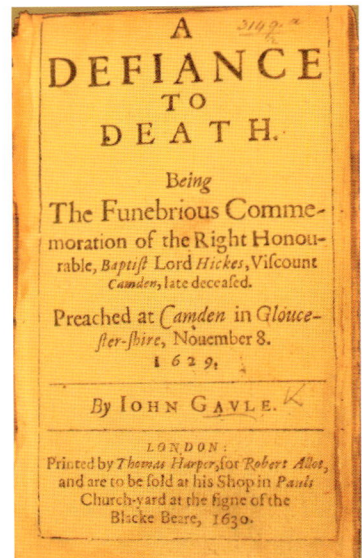

"He was a man (as it is well knowne) worshipfully borne, religiously educated, wisely instructed, honorably promoted; A man happy in a loyall wife, joyful in virtuous children, prosperous in worldly wealth. …For his Charity, it is well noted, where ever he had anything to doe, the first thing he did, was alwaies to doe good. Besides his oft, and private almes, his light moreover shines in publique, and both in City, and country, men may see his good works."
A Defiance to Death, John Gaule, 1629

The Hicks monument possibly by Nicholas Stone in the Gainsborough Chapel, St James' Church

O happy Campden,
you possess great riches and the body of your finest patron,

who restored the Lordship
and added new blossoms of honour to your land.

He has embellished your town
with many buildings and flourishing gardens...

Translation from the Latin; from the inscription on the Hicks' monument,
St James' Church, Chipping Campden

"The Theater of his Hospitality"

(From *The Elements of Architecture*, Sir Henry Wooten, 1624)

The Buildings of Campden House

A building boom was sweeping England in the early 17th century. Successful merchants like Baptist Hicks had attained wealth and honours, but to be truly established they needed property, and the more magnificent the better. Land meant security and status so it is no coincidence that there was this frenzy of housebuilding. Hicks joined in the boom enthusiastically with three major building projects on the go from about 1610 to 1616; the new Middlesex Sessions House, a mansion in Kensington also called Campden House, and Campden House in Chipping Campden. (To avoid confusion, where the name Campden House is used throughout this book, it refers to Campden House, Chipping Campden. The London house is referred to as Campden House, Kensington.) With a fortune made from trade and moneylending, Hicks would have wanted to show himself as a bona fide member of the elite, so his houses had to be beautiful and refined, an expression of his own *quality*.

Holland House (formerly known as Cope Castle) was owned by Sir Walter Cope, one of the new breed of successful men in Jacobean England. Hicks is said to have won land next to Holland House from Cope in a game of chance. He built a house on that land, also called Campden House. John Wykeham Archer, 1857.
British Museum

The influence of the Renaissance had travelled across Europe but by the time it reached England, the classical ideal had been diluted and was being used in conjunction with some very unclassical ornamentation. Both styles were embraced by English housebuilders. Jacobean architecture became defined by complexity; decoration and symbols, gables and towers, bay windows, confining walls and courtyards were all popular features. But classical elements like columns and capitals, round arched loggia, garden pavilions and an overall symmetry were also incorporated. The result was an exuberant, eclectic, style of architecture. Our knowledge of Campden House is limited, but we do know that all these developments found a place here.

Architecture as we would recognise it began to develop as a profession in the second half of the 16th century. Previously the work had been done by skilled masons, but now a small group of men emerged who were producing house plans, men such as Robert Smythson, William Arnold, Robert Lyminge, and of particular significance to the story of Campden House, John Thorpe (c.1563-1655). Most of what we know of Thorpe comes from a folio of drawings he made, known as the *Book of Architecture,* which contains some clues about the origins of Campden House. Only a few of the plans can be attributed to built houses, notably Aston Hall in Birmingham, and many are copies of other people's work, but the *Book of Architecture* does contain a set of plans for a *'mr Hix'*, one of which has been identified as Campden House, Kensington.

Beaufort House. In the distance the three great houses of Kensington can be seen on the hills above; Holland House, Campden House and Nottingham House (now Kensington Palace). Jan Kip, 1707 British Museum

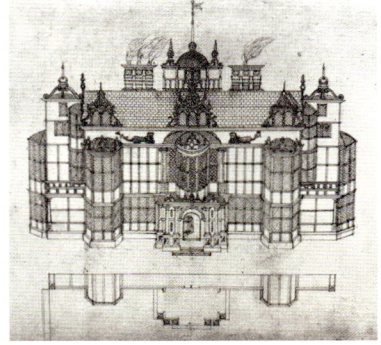

Campden House, Kensington, built around the same time as Campden House, Chipping Campden. Given that we know so little about the latter, this other house of Hicks' offers important clues such as his taste, the style he favoured and the architect he employed. It was described as 'a very noble pile, and finished with all the art the architects of that time were masters of'. *The house stood three storeys high, with large bay windows and corner turrets topped with ogee domes (altered in this later picture). An elaborately carved entrance porch, typically Jacobean in style, had Hicks' arms sculpted upon it and a pierced parapet surmounted the entire façade. The external walls were covered in ornament which was gradually lost until they were covered in stucco. Plaster ceilings and painted windows were decorated with the arms of Hicks and his sons-in law. In the Great Chamber there was an enormous oak mantelpiece with six Corinthian columns supporting a pediment and decorated with grotesque devices, the whole held by two finely carved caryatid figures. The house was destroyed by fire in 1862.*
Copperplate etching, 1795. Kensington Central Library

Plate 44 from John Thorpe's Book of Architecture *has been identified as Campden House, Kensington. The execution did differ from this; the drawing shows a timber house, whereas it was built in red brick with stone finishings.*
John Soane Museum

Another Thorpe drawing (see overleaf) shows a floor plan for a house with an 'H' shape and it has been suggested that this is an early drawing for Campden House in Chipping Campden. Above this plan is a miniature sketch of possibly the same house with several revisions. This thumbnail sketch bears a striking resemblance to the remains of Campden House, and significantly, to the plan of the house revealed by the geophysical survey. Although there must always be an element of uncertainty, this drawing could be a rough sketch for Campden House.

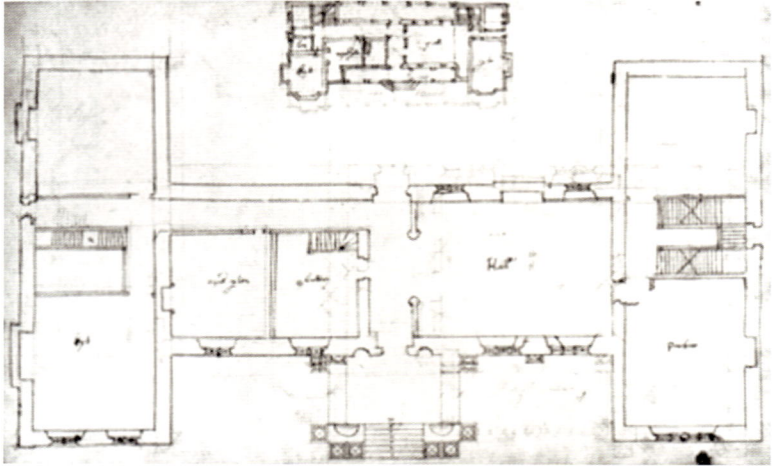

Plans from John Thorpe's **Book of Architecture** *for 'Mr Hix'. The larger drawing could be an early plan for Campden House and the small sketch enlarged here on the right a later development of it.*
John Soane Museum

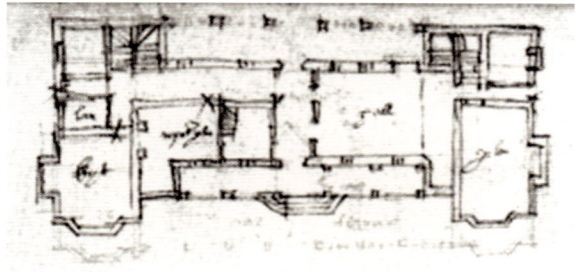

Detail of geophysical survey of Campden House by CCHS, 2014. The grid lines are 20m square and the blue lines indicate the extant ruin. Some of the ground floor room layout is revealed, as are remnants of the surrounding garden walls. The 'u' shaped feature on the right of this image was found during excavation to post-date the House.

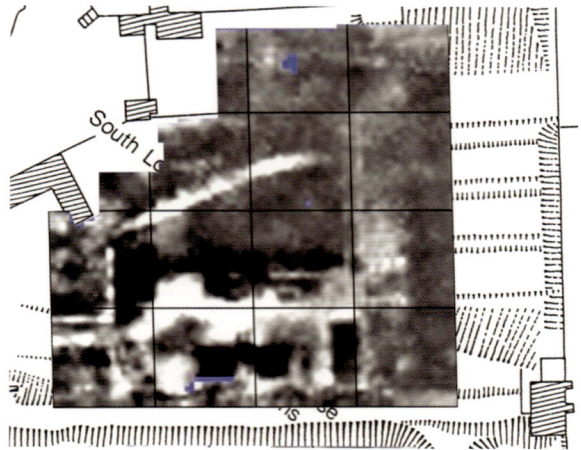

The Bird's-Eye Views (see inside front cover)

The link between Thorpe and Campden House is also supported by the similarity of the Thorpe plans to the few images we have of the House. None are contemporary, but there are six bird's-eye views, produced at different times. The later ones were probably copied from the earlier, all of the south façade of the House and Gardens. The earliest drawings could have relied upon a lost original. Despite inconsistencies and inaccuracies, they are essentially correct with regard to the layout of the site and the extant remains. Even allowing for their flaws, they represent an invaluable source of information about the House, the ancillary buildings, the Gardens and the wider landscape.

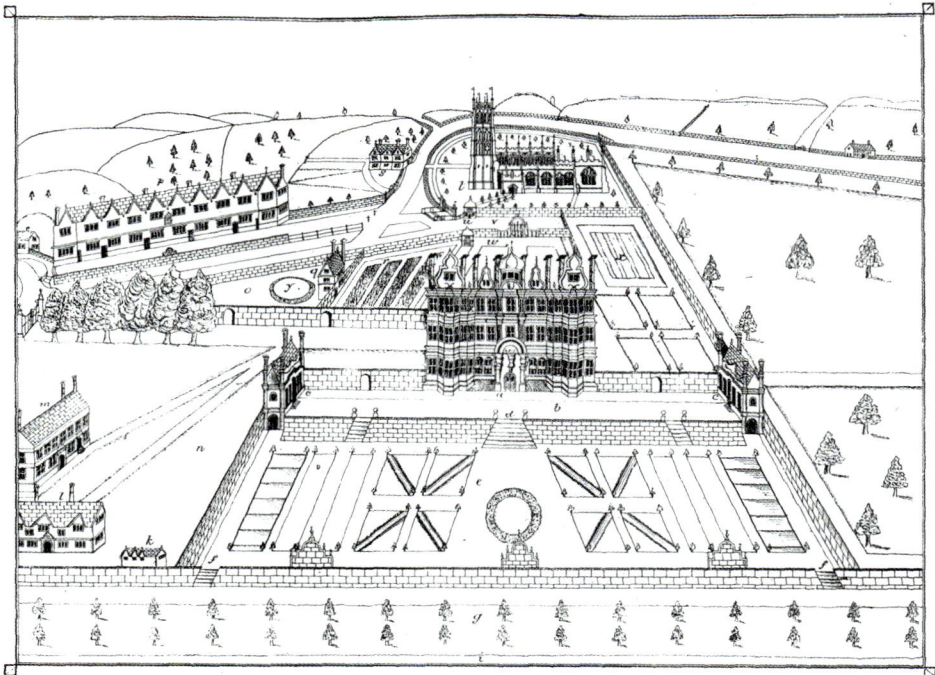

BIRDSEYE VIEW OF CAMPDEN HOUSE, BURNT DOWN IN THE YEAR OF NASEBY, 1645 (from an old drawing).

References—*a* The house. *b* The terrass walk. *c* The banquiting house. *d* The garden staires. *e* The great garden. *f* The orchart staires. *g* The great orchart. *i* The long canal. *k* The coach-house. *l* The brew-house. *m* The stables. *n* The stable court. *o* The henn yard. *p* The hospital. *q* The laundry. *r* The bleach garden. *s* The parsonage house. *t* The church. *u* The porter's lodge. *v* The outward court. *w* The great court. *x* The garden court. *y* The pond.

The Rushen Bird's-Eye. This illustration appeared in Percy Rushen's History of Campden, 1899.

The Gatehouse

The Gatehouse mattered because it was the introduction to the House, a foretaste of its quality. Even today the distinctive curvaceous profile conveys a sense of occasion and is a key component of the most celebrated historic vista in Chipping Campden. This is Jacobean mannerism in its truest sense and Hicks created a theatrical introduction to his House with this decorative flight of fancy. Built into the new boundary wall, it stood at right angles to the House. It must have made a wonderful spectacle, with the magnificent church of St. James' on one side and the House on the other.

The Gatehouse, Campden House

The role of Gatehouses had been changing. In medieval times they had been defensive structures, but by the early 17th century, whilst still controlling access to the house, a growing sense of security transformed them from the architecture of intimidation to that of display. They became lower and broader, often with paired lodges rather than a single building. Campden's Gatehouse epitomises this transition. Two symmetrical Lodges, built in Cotswold ashlar with mullioned windows and beautifully constructed stone ogee domes are linked by a screen with a curvilinear profile. The two pierced finials on this gabled curtain wall or screen are in fact chimney flues, typical of Jacobean ingenuity. The Lodges themselves are quite simple buildings, not large, probably accommodation for the porter and his family and other estate staff. All the bird's-eye images show the two Lodges standing independently, not linked by the screen. Perhaps this had been the designer's original intention. Gatehouses were often one of the final elements of a plan to be completed in these great housebuilding schemes, so it is possible that the distinctive curtain wall is a slightly later addition. The stylistic differences could suggest a later date. It is not possible to be conclusive, and making the challenge even more difficult are the numerous alterations made to the Lodges over the years, some of them, such as the corner chimney in the south Lodge, very early.

The Hicks coat of arms is displayed on the central tympanum. The arched carriageway is not wide and it is unlikely that it was commonly used, probably reserved for special occasions and important visitors. An alternative entrance at the corner of Church Street and Calf Lane was in a more convenient position, suggesting that it was the entrance normally used.

Overall the Gatehouse has a combination of classical forms and gothic flamboyance and yet the effect is one of great charm. Many of these buildings have been lost, vulnerable to demolition as the fashion for open parkland swept them away. This example at Chipping Campden is an outstanding survivor, there are no buildings in the Cotswold vernacular that resemble it – it is unique.

The Great Court

Passing through the carriageway and turning south, the Great Court is entered. The bird's-eyes show a walled and gated inner courtyard, but none of the archaeological investigations found any evidence to support this and we know that some of the features in the bird's-eyes are unreliable. Although these walled inner courts were common at this time, it would have made the turn from the Gatehouse extremely tight. More probable was one large courtyard laid out in front of the House and walled on either side (geophysical survey did reveal remnants of some of these enclosing walls). Hicks built the wall that encloses the churchyard today, presumably as part of his design, and perhaps to preclude the need for an inner court. The doorway in this wall allowing him private access to the churchyard is now filled in but it can still be clearly discerned. Walls flanking the Great Court may have linked up up to walls either side of the House that themselves linked to the Banqueting Houses. The bird's-eyes show a drive leading up to the front door with two rectangular beds of grass on either side. (The Court Barn is a later addition, post-dating the destruction of the House).

The House

On entering the Gatehouse today and turning south, the surviving fragment of Campden House stands forlorn, looking down to the river and the Cotswold hills beyond. A length of ashlar stone wall, fire reddened on one side, 10 metres long and reaching up to a little above the first floor windowsill remains. It is part of the south facing, garden front of the House. Enough of the southwest arm is preserved to show the jamb of a bay window, two ground floor windows and the remnants of two first floor windows. There are two blocked short windows, ostensibly for a basement; study of their reverse side suggests they may have been blind windows, perhaps added to enhance the symmetry of the façade. The ruin ends to the east with a column shaft, capital and moulded base and part of an arch with Arabesque strapwork. This is all that survives and is therefore a most significant piece of evidence when trying to piece together how the House may have looked. The bird's-eyes show a house three storeys high with additional attic rooms. It was approximately 40 metres wide and 20-25 metres deep.

The surviving fragment of Campden House. Part of a bay window and the first column and arch of the Loggia can still be seen.
Jesse Taylor/CCHS

Campden House was certainly very fine, but one of the first observations to make is that it was not particularly large when considered in the context of other mansions of the time. This was never Hicks' primary residence. He remained firmly rooted in London, with a house in the City and another in the fields of Kensington. Writing to his brother, Hicks says *I wish that my wife were as well pleased in the country, but it avails not to wish it'* and there is no evidence to suggest that he spent much time in Chipping Campden. Given the style of the property, it was probably somewhere for short stays and entertainment, more in the manner of a lodge or summer house. The beauty, even glamour, of this House would convey the possession of money and power. (It is interesting to compare the style of Hicks' tomb with the buildings of Campden House. In reality the House was probably out of fashion soon after it was finished.)

Hicks was not a member of the aristocracy so a larger house may not have been deemed appropriate, but to a great extent the size of the House was determined by the site. Originally the ground would have sloped naturally down to the river, but quantities of earth were moved to construct a series of terraces leading down to the lower gardens. The largest terrace was the highest, close by the church, and the flat area created there is where the House was placed. During the restoration of the East Banqueting House in 1990, medieval tiles were found in rubble adjacent to the building, at a considerable depth. Soil and rubble had clearly been brought, possibly from the earlier Manor House, to create the necessary stability for the terraces and buildings. Excavations of the House in 2017 and 2018 revealed that piles of stone rubble were laid to make a more secure platform to build on than the freshly moved soil (the full extent of this rubble layer was not determined, but it was certainly substantial).

Excavations of the House went to a depth of 2 metres, but did not determine the extent of the rubble layer that was interpreted as a 'platform' upon which the house was constructed. One medieval tile was discovered here, suggesting again that at least some of that debris came from an earlier building.
CCHS, 2018

33

No documentation relating to the construction or early years of the House has been found, and even sources from succeeding centuries are scarce. One significant account we do have is by the antiquarian Ralph Bigland (1712-1784), who visited the *'magnificent pile'* in the early 1780s. He quotes from what he says was *'an accurate plan and elevation, still extant'*, describing *'this most sumptuous house with accompaniments of magnificence'* and he gives the figure of £29,000 as the cost to build it, a fortune at that time. (His source for that figure is not known but possibly it was the plan he refers to). He describes the House: *'It consisted of four Fronts, the principal one being towards the Garden, upon the Grand Terras; at each Angle was a lateral Projection of some Feet, with spacious Bow Windows; in the Centre a Portico, with a Series of Columns of the five Orders (as in the Schools at Oxford), and an open Corridore. The Parapet was finished with Pediments of a capricious Taste, and the Chimneys were twisted Pillars with Corinthian Capitals. A very capricious Dome issued from the Roof, which was regularly illuminated for the Direction of Travellers during the Night. This immense Building was enriched with Frizes and Entablatures, most profusely sculptured'*. Whilst this account must be read with some circumspection as the House was long gone by the time Bigland visited, if based on an extant plan it does contain some intriguing clues. For example, columned *'portico'* or loggia were a continental feature that had become popular, seen at some of the best contemporary houses such as Hatfield House and Holland House, and it seems Campden may have had one at the front and the rear.

Hatfield House, Hertfordshire, 1611. Built by Sir Robert Cecil with whom Hicks and his brother Michael had close ties. Although Hatfield is a true Prodigy House, it shares many characteristics with Campden House and Gardens. The Loggia has been filled in, but in the 17th century, it would have stood open to the Terrace, as it did at Campden.
Alan Engelhardt

Thorpe's plan shows a Loggia of two arches either side of the front door. Given that there is no certain knowledge about this north façade, it was one of the areas focused on during the excavations. The archaeological remains were fragmentary and it soon became obvious that the site had been systematically cleared. However, the foundations of walls that were located, when studied in conjunction with the geophysical survey, do support this. Indeed although the surviving archaeological evidence of the House is imprecise, nothing that was discovered during the excavations contradict the Thorpe plan.

The Jacobean period was a transitional time for architecture. Old medieval plans were changing but some aspects endured. In earlier buildings it was common for the main entrance not to be placed centrally, but by this time a symmetrical façade was more desirable. So at nearby Chastleton House for example, the architect has retained the older fashion of an off centre main entrance but also incorporated the new by tucking it into the side of a bay, thus creating the illusion of a symmetrical front. At Campden however, the central entrance design has been fully embraced.

Chastleton House, Gloucestershire, 1612. The front door is located inside the left bay, making the elevation symmetrical whilst retaining the tradition of an off centre entrance. Celucci

Clearly the intention of the Gatehouse was to set the scene and the theatricality would have continued at the front entrance. The Hicks coat of arms can still be seen around Chipping Campden, on the Market Hall, the Almshouses and the Gatehouse. From this we can infer that much use would have been made of it on and in his House. One can imagine it forming the centrepiece of an elaborately decorated entrance porch, emblazoned above the door. Heraldry, emblems and armorial crests were ubiquitous, used on almost every available surface; over-mantles, doorways, friezes, wainscoting, ceilings and window glass. They served to proclaim not only the ancestry of the owner, but also their allegiances and marriage alliances. In his house in Kensington, we know that the arms of Hicks' sons-in-law were displayed in painted window glass, in addition to his own, and it is likely that they were here too. As we have seen, Hicks was closely associated with life in the Court and he may well have had royal coats of arms added in deference to the King.

Mottoes and emblems known as 'devices' and figures from myth and allegory were extremely popular. Although they can seem incomprehensible to us now, many were understood in their day. Others took more ingenuity to understand and it was a popular game to try and decipher the hidden codes and messages. In some cases, the 'device' was embedded in the design of the building, a trick Thorpe obviously enjoyed, judging by the evidence of his plans in the *Book of Architecture*. In the possible sketch of Campden House, the letter H can be discerned and the Almshouses Hicks built in Chipping Campden form the the letter 'I' in deference to James, a time when a capital 'J' was often written as an 'I'.

The window of the Great Chamber at Montacute House in Somerset displays the arms of families connected to the Phelips by marriage.

Tour of the House

Our knowledge of the House interior is obviously limited but by piecing together the available information, we have imagined a walk around it to try and conjure the look and feel of its glory days. Staying with the Thorpe plan, on entering the front door there is a wide, straight corridor terminating at the door leading to the south Loggia and onto the main Terrace Walk. If accurate, a spectacular view of the terraces and the Cotswold hills beyond would have been visible immediately. This would have been unusual for an early 17th century house, giving it the lighter airy feel in keeping with a place of entertainment and relaxation but not usually associated with houses of the period.

The floor was probably a combination of stone and wood. Most of the walls would have been covered in richly carved wood paneling as the fashion for oak wainscoted rooms still prevailed. These panels were quite small and in the best houses, very

Campden House, Kensington. This image dates from the 19th century when the house was a girls' school, but the original Jacobean interior decoration clearly remains unchanged.
Kensington Central Library

elaborately carved and arranged in sections divided by wood pilasters which could run the entire room height. This is just the style that can be seen in the only surviving image of the interior of Campden House, Kensington and therefore a good indication of the decoration here.

Once through the door, the largest room encountered on the ground floor would have been the Great Hall. For centuries, the Hall had been the axis of the house, and it remained an important space. All visitors would have passed through it but its purpose had changed and it was in decline. Servants continued to eat there in some households, deceased family members were laid out there before the funeral (perhaps Hicks' body was placed here after its journey

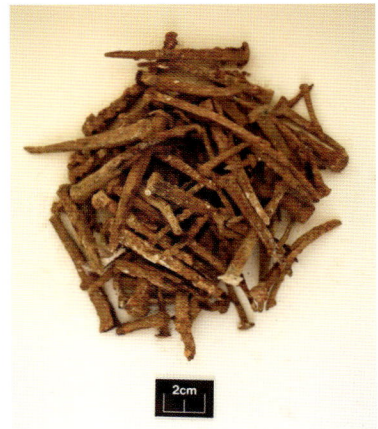

Hundreds of handmade nails of all sizes were recovered in the excavations, indicating that the quantity of wood used in the building and fitting of the house was enormous.

37

from London, prior to interment in St James' Church) and it was still the setting for festivities, but the introduction of other rooms like the Parlour, the Great Chamber and the Library were creating alternative spaces for a whole range of activities.

Rooms commonly remained interconnecting but the relatively new notion of privacy was gaining popularity, and with it came new rooms. On the ground floor a Parlour was becoming essential, a smaller withdrawing room more comfortable and intimate than the Hall. Thorpe's plan has two Parlours, one for summer and one for winter, the latter located by the Kitchen for extra warmth. The Summer Parlour had a stepped bay window to the south and a smaller bay to the east, an arrangement mirrored on the west side of the House. The better family rooms were located at the old 'high' end of the Hall on the east of the building, and at the other 'low' side were the service rooms: kitchen, buttery and pantry. In Thorpe's plan, the Kitchen is in the large room overlooking the garden on the south west side of the House. Given this favourable location, it might seem too good a room in which to place the utilitarian kitchen, but study of the extant ruin shows there had probably been a

large fireplace here, much as one would expect to find in a kitchen of the time. Soon such rooms would invariably be located in the basement, but at this time they were still commonly on the ground floor. Excavations suggested some subterranean rooms, not basements of any significant size, probably with a reduced ceiling height perhaps for storage, cold rooms, wine etc. The site does have many changes in level, and at the west side of the House towards the ancillary buildings, the ground falls away steeply which could allow for basement rooms but no excavations were undertaken in this area. Either way, the domestic rooms were placed on the west side of the House, most easily accessible to the separate service buildings where deliveries could be conveniently made. The geophysical survey revealed a series of walls here, dividing the superior elements of the House and Garden from the domestic areas.

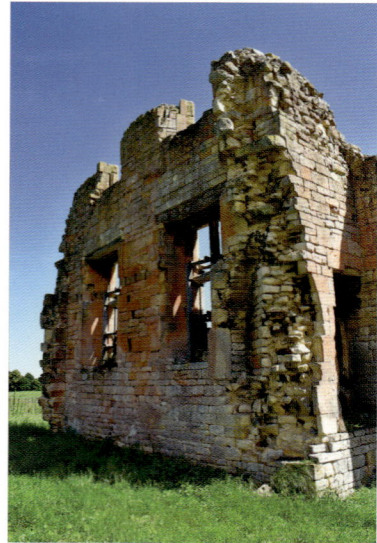

The interior side of the ruin showing the distinctive pink of the burnt stone and what is probably the remains of a large fireplace.
Keyna Doran 2018

The Canterbury Quadrangle, St. John's College, Oxford. Masons from Chipping Campden worked on this building and may have created something similar at Campden House.
Andrew Shiva

A significant feature of the ground floor, and one which we can be sure existed, is the Loggia. Although the presence of a Loggia to the north of the House remains speculation, there was certainly one to the south, overlooking the gardens. It may have resembled the Canterbury Quadrangle at St John's College, Oxford, referred to by Ralph Bigland as *'a series of columns of the five orders (as in the schools at Oxford)'*. The College records of 1636 include details of the construction of this Quadrangle and they mention the White family, skilled stonemasons from Chipping Campden, who may also have worked on Campden House.

The ruin ends with a column and part of an arch from the Loggia. Assuming that the House stood centrally between the Banqueting Houses, it probably incorporated an arcade of four bays, two on either side of the central door. The Thorpe plan has a wide flight of steps leading down to the Terrace. A true classical innovation, the Loggia was a sheltered space neither inside nor out. Here at Campden its elevated position meant that it commanded fine south facing views over the Great Parterre to the further reaches of the Garden and the countryside beyond.

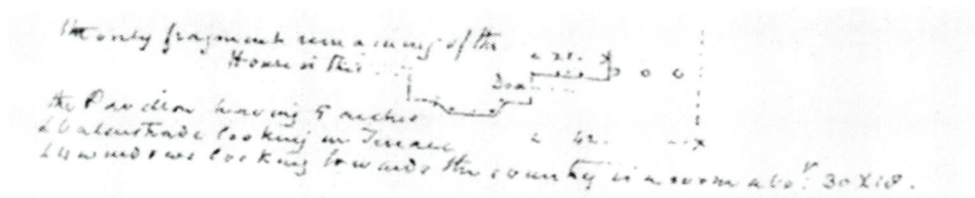

This sketch plan of the ruins was drawn by C.R. Cockerell in 1825. He has noted the base of three pillars from the Loggia, today there is only one.
RIBA Drawings Collection

Back inside the House and to another feature where an ambitious builder could make a statement, the Staircase. Hicks had a good supply of quality local stone, so it is possible he used it to build his stair. It would certainly have been a fabulous addition, but it would have been uncommon, the vast majority at this time being made from wood. The cantilevered stair, a technical breakthrough of the late Elizabethan age, would have been the height of fashion, and whether of wood or stone, Hicks may have wanted one. Here was another place for every surface to be covered with lavish decoration. Stairs were popular locations for carved figures from myth and legend, for heraldry and for more personal additions.

If the veracity of the Thorpe sketch is to be relied upon, there were two staircases of significant size at Campden placed either side of the front entrance. These could have been built within towers located on the front of the building. Another minor staircase is shown in the small room adjacent to the Winter Parlour.

Moving up the stairs, it must be remembered that we have no information about the layout of the upper floors, so we have to rely on secondary sources for our understanding of them. By this time, the best rooms had moved upstairs, and the grandest of all was the Great Chamber. This was the most fabulous room in the House, used for dining, dancing and entertainment.

Robert Cecil is said to have had the figure of his favourite plantsman, John Tradescant, carved at the top of his great stair at Hatfield House.

It was an essential space for anyone with pretentions to status and taste and as such is a good location to consider the interior decoration.

The only certain information we have about the interior and contents of the House comes from the wills of Baptist and Elizabeth Hicks, and from the archaeological excavations. Both have provided tantalizing insights into the House of the early 17th century. The wills list an array of household items that must have been in the House including various items of furniture, plate, linen and fire irons. We do not know if the contents were removed during the Civil War, however Lady Juliana, Hicks' daughter, put a figure of £15,000 on their value. Whether that is an accurate assessment or not, it is reasonable to suppose that Hicks spared no expense on furnishings.

The Great Chamber, Aston Hall, a building we know was designed by John Thorpe, the possible architect of Campden House
Joseph Nash, 1870

Detail from an Arras tapestry, **Adam Tilling the Ground,** *1550*
Wawel Royal Castle National Art Collection

As a merchant whose trade was in fine fabrics, Hicks had a web of contacts stretching across the Continent and perhaps beyond, and he would have wanted the very best for himself. His House was no parochial country squire's residence. It was plush, rich and metropolitan. Rooms were hung with gorgeous tapestries of silk, gold and silver thread. Arras in northern France was the centre for the production of the finest tapestries and in his will, Hicks refers to his *'arras hangings'*. They literally wove a story, combining extraordinary craftsmanship with Biblical and popular dramatic narratives such as Spenser's *Faerie Queene*. They would have been wildly expensive and eminently desirable items.

41

Pieces of carved stone found during the excavations could have come from elaborately decorated fireplaces. Human figures, like this carved face found during the excavations, were a popular theme. They are sometimes referred to as 'grotesques'. The fragment of a hand was also recovered, its size suggesting that the form was almost life-size.

Numerous fragments of decorated plaster, some of it painted, were discovered during the excavations. A fish scale motif seems to have recurred, perhaps as a frieze, as did faces and swirling patterns of leaves and flowers. The quantity of plaster recovered suggests it formed an important element of the decorative scheme.

As the Great Chamber had replaced the Hall as the main entertaining space, it would have had the finest fireplace. Undoubtedly it was very decorative, probably top-heavy and covered in sculpture, columns, obelisks and ornament, again with that eclectic mix of gothic and classical. They were status symbols, and another convenient focal point on which to locate heraldry.

A lighter atmosphere in the rooms had become desirable, hence the popularity of white plasterwork ceilings. Their design was inventive, with countless varieties of style and subject matter, and they demonstrated an extraordinary and often extremely delicate craftsmanship. Magnificent pendants strengthened the structure of the ceiling and added grandeur.

Detail drawn from the plaster frieze in the West Banqueting House by Percy D. Smith in the 1890s

A strapwork plaster ceiling from Campden House, Kensington. It has been suggested that the Kensington ceilings of were made by James Leigh, master craftsman to the King, and responsible for some of the magnificent ceilings at Hatfield. Hicks may have employed him to work here at Campden House.
Kensington Central Library

Plaster ceilings added to a sense of light and space, but it was the windows that really made the difference, separating these Jacobean spaces from many of their Tudor and medieval forerunners. All of the bird's–eyes depict a house with lots of windows and they would have created a spectacular effect, both inside and out. Bay windows were popular as they let in more light and created pleasant places to sit within a room. The geophysical survey, the Thorpe drawing and the Bigland description all have bay windows to each of the four elevations of the House, and the ruin has the remnant of one. Windows were expensive and so were an obvious display of wealth. The glass glinting in the sun would have created a memorable impression of the house from some distance.

Although the pieces of glass discovered during the excavations were small in size, they were very large in number. Close study of them showed that many pieces were cut into intricate shapes.
Contemporary books such as **A booke of sundry draughtes principaly serving for glasiers** *by Walter Gigge, 1615, describe the decoration and ornament of windows and illustrate the wide choice of glass patterns available to those who could afford them (above right). The numerous fragments of fine cut glass and the window lead found at the site are evidence of Campden House's sophisticated glazing.*

These Jacobean houses weren't filled with furniture in the way later houses were. What furniture there was, was dark, heavy and ornate. The wills of Baptist and Elizabeth Hicks list chairs, stools, tables *'of all sorts'*, forms (i.e. benches) and cupboards. As with architecture, the 17th century would see great changes in interior design, but when Campden House was built Tudor fashions still prevailed and oak remained the most commonly used wood.

Oriental 'Turkey' rugs were used as much to cover furniture as the floor, and along with the rich tapestries they created sumptuous spaces. In her will, Lady Hicks

This pulpit was donated by Baptist Hicks in 1612 and remains in St James' Church, Chipping Campden today. It illustrates the kind of wood carving that would have proliferated in the House.
Rachel Cunynghame

bequeaths a *'long Persia carpet being ten yards long and three yards half and half quarter broad'*, and although we do not know which of their properties housed this carpet, it would have been a fabulously expensive and luxurious item, demonstrating the lavish lifestyle they enjoyed. The Great Chamber at Campden House would presumably have had a large Court Cupboard upon which to display the plate. In his will, Hicks left *'all my silver and white silver plate'*, pewter, gilt and brass, saucers, spoons and candlesticks, salt cellars, and *'dishes of all sorts both great and small'*. His *'great silver voider* [a large dish] *and great silver knife'* he bequeathed to the Company of Mercers.

Bedchambers had become increasingly fine, although it was still quite common at this time for them to be shared. Beds had elaborate carved decoration and hangings of velvet and other rich materials. Beds and bedsteads of all sorts feature in the Hicks' wills, along with details of the accompanying linen. Campden House probably did not have a large number of bedchambers; there would have been at least a couple that were very grand on the first floor for Hicks and his principal guest, perhaps with closets. The remainder would have been on the second floor. Some servants slept where they worked, others would have had small shared rooms, probably in the attic rooms seen in the bird's-eyes. The Banqueting Houses offered the option of additional sleeping quarters and staff may also have lodged there.

The final room of architectural significance was the Long Gallery. It could have been on any of the upper floors, but given what we know of the size of Campden House, it was probably on the second floor, offering panoramic views of the gardens. This room, often running the entire length of the House, had developed as an indoor space for walking, exercise being considered very important. Big enough to be able to gather in small groups and commune privately, it was another very impressive room with a superbly decorative plaster ceiling. With the possible

45

The pottery finds from the House excavations included sherds of the Rhenish stoneware ubiquitous in the 17th century. Some are from Bellarmine jugs, with their distinctive salt glaze (right), which were commonly used drinking vessels imported from the Low Countries and the Rhineland.

A wide variety of pottery sherds were excavated, including several pieces of slipware; this photograph shows a selection from the assemblage.

Excavation finds also included some gilded glass and fragments of delicately decorated Venetian glass (above left). The glass (above right) is an example of how the intact vessel may have looked. This was tableware of the very highest status, prohibitively expensive and extremely precious, and is another indication of the opulent manner in which Hicks lived and the sums of money he was spending.
CCHS, 2017

exception of the stairs, it was the only room where paintings were hung in any significant number. As in Elizabethan times, they were usually portraits. Lady Hicks does leave pictures in her will, although the only one she specifies is *'one great picture of the transfiguration of Christ'* hanging in the Kensington house. The Long Gallery may also have been the location for other extravagant items listed in the wills; the wind instruments, statues and looking glasses would all undoubtedly have added to the opulent atmosphere.

The Long Gallery, Aston Hall
Tony Higsett

Turning finally to the roof, the local stone at Westington is too porous for roof slates, so another source would have been needed. Some were found in the excavations but not enough to determine whether they had covered the whole building. When restoring the Banqueting Houses, the Landmark Trust refers to their *'ruined stone roof'* and it could be argued that all the buildings would have been roofed in the same way. It is possible that lead was used, although no evidence was found for this. The 17th century was a heyday for all kinds of leadwork; inventive plumbers and glaziers were making conduits for water supplies and fountains, fancy glazing for windows, down pipes and elaborate rainwater heads. The Conduit House on Westington Hill was built by Hicks to capture the water from springs there. It was transported via lead pipes under the ground to the House. Stone culverts survive in the fields adjacent to the house, and fragments of lead pipe have been found next to Lady Juliana's Gateway and under nearby fields. The date of this pipe has not been established and no lead piping has been recovered near the House, but given the sophisticated engineering of the Garden and the expense of the House, it is very likely that clean running water was made available. The Almshouses, also built by Hicks, had fresh water provided by a communal tap.

The Conduit House, Chipping Campden by F. L. Griggs, 1919

There are numerous references in later documents relating to the water supply, especially repairs to it, although they offer no significant details. The Almshouses and Vicarage continued to be supplied by this source into the 20th century.

As the roof was no longer the site for battlements and defences, it was freed up to become another 'secret' place for yet more pleasure. One popular addition was a Roof Walk taking advantage of the view. We cannot know if there was one here, but Bigland's description of the parapets 'finished with pediments of a capricious taste' and 'twisted chimneys', presumably matching the Banqueting Houses, suggests a roofline busy with decoration.

Dutch or Flemish gables were soon to die out, but they were still popular at the time Campden House was built. It was usual for a decorative scheme to be continued throughout an estate's plan, making the Banqueting Houses and Gatehouse important when trying to understand how the House may have looked.

The rooflines of the Banqueting Houses are extremely decorative and probably emulate the main House. The drawing is a detail from sketches of pierced strapwork in John Thorpe's **Book of Architecture** *and are similar to what we can see at Campden.*

From what we know of these buildings and of Baptist Hicks himself, we can assume there was an embellished façade with ornate chimneys and pierced strapwork rather than the plainer, more reserved look seen at Chastleton House. The *'profusely sculptured frizes and entablatures'* on the external walls would have been typical of the most expensive Jacobean style.

Another design feature that looked to the past was the ogee dome. Also soon to fall out of fashion, at Campden they can be seen on the Gatehouse Lodges, and on towers at St James' Church, added by Hicks. Given their proximity, ogees probably formed part of the Campden

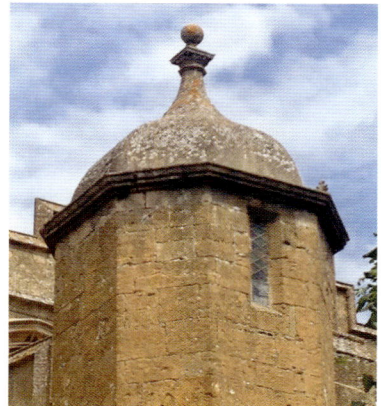

Two ogee domes added by Hicks to the nearby Church suggest a similar feature would have been included on his House.

49

House roof design. Thorpe's sketch suggests that the two stairwells at the front of the building were housed in towers and they would almost certainly have been topped with domes and decorative finials. Although replaced in the 18th century, Campden House, Kensington originally had ogee domes atop its corner turrets so we can be reasonably confident they were also a feature on this Campden House.

Much of what we know about Campden House remains guesswork, for example was the Palladian style Lantern a reality? Bigland says it was *'illuminated for the direction of travelers during the night'* and it features in all the bird's-eyes. It was a striking feature in houses such as Aston Hall, Hatfield House and Blickling Hall, all Campden's contemporaries; moreover, John Thorpe was particularly fond of adding a *'capricious'* lantern to his designs. As Hicks was orchestrating a landscape to impress from a distance, it is likely that he would have wanted this feature that could be seen for miles. From the Gatehouse to the top of the roof, whoever planned this House was a true master of display.

Drawings of lantern designs in **The Book of Architecture** *by John Thorpe*

The Banqueting Houses

In the pursuit of gracious living, creating an exterior as exquisite as the interior would have been essential. The feature that did this more than any other was the Banqueting House. They had become popular during the 16th century, following the French fashion, and by the turn of the 17th century had become ever more intricate and sophisticated. The name derives from their original use as a place for al fresco dining. Despite their name, this would not have been a banquet as we know it today, but rather a place where 'conceited dishes' were consumed often following a sumptuous dinner, in a more intimate setting. The fancy jellies, marzipans, meringues and sweetmeats, the decorated game and fish *'made for shew only'* gave the event a theatrical air, all accompanied by spiced and mulled wines. How everything looked was at least, if not more important than how it tasted and only the most select of guests would be entertained in this rarified environment.

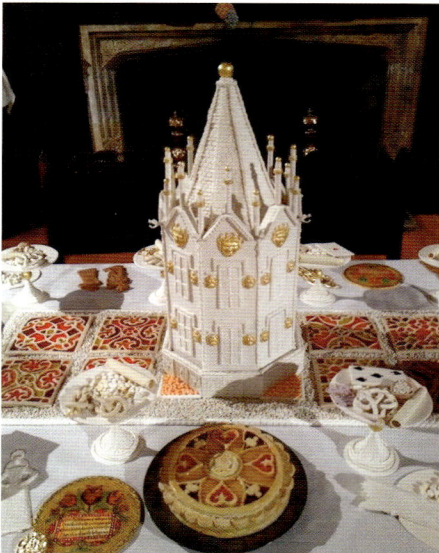

Reconstruction of a Banquet of Sweetmeats with an edible banqueting house in an edible knot garden. Marchpane garden 'knots' are filled with flowerbeds made from fruit pastes and surrounded by gravel walks of caraway comfits. There are also edible sugar plates or 'tazze' filled with 'jumbals' (biscuits), sugar playing cards, gilt gingerbread figures and other 'banqueting stuffes'.
Bowes Museum

Over time the Banqueting House became increasingly important for providing architectural focus to the garden, and a view was an essential element. Inviting and complex prospects were an integral part of the Jacobean exterior, and the ingenious design of these little houses made them the perfect place to indulge whilst enjoying beautiful vistas. Like Gatehouses, Banqueting Houses have been vulnerable over the centuries and many have been lost. Those at Chipping Campden are perhaps the finest surviving examples in the country. In true Jacobean style they mislead the eye, appearing to be identical from the Terrace Walk where they flank the House to the

51

From the Terrace Walk the Banqueting Houses appear to be identical buildings. The East Banqueting House is shown prior to restoration, the open arcades giving some impression of how it had originally looked.
Jesse Taylor/CCHS

The corresponding arches in the West Banqueting House have been infilled with stone, much of it burnt.

east and the west, but in reality they are two very different buildings. Both are distinctive and decorative and they were an important feature not only of the garden, but of the lifestyle that Hicks was pursuing. Two and three storeys high, they are unusually substantial, and the craftsmanship is of a very high standard. They were clearly built to complement the House and in their design, ornamentation and stylistic eclecticism they are definitively Jacobean buildings. Barley sugar chimneys twist up from each corner, gables are ornate and the parapets have pierced strapwork. As we have seen elsewhere, classical and local vernacular styles are combined, and the result is delightful. Despite the alterations and changes of use that have been made over the centuries, these buildings remain exceptional.

Viewed from the back, the differences between the two Banqueting Houses are clearly seen. The East (top) is three storeys, the land falling away steeply here, the West (left) is two storeys.

Originally, both houses were airy loggias open to the Terrace Walk. Investigations by the Landmark Trust have determined that there was no internal stair at this level, confirming their purpose as independent garden arbours. Although now glazed or infilled with stone, enough remains to convey an impression of how they must have looked when they were luxurious arcades.

The East Banqueting House is built into the bank at the edge of the levelled area where the main House stood. This bank is so steep that the Banqueting House rises to three storeys high, although it appears from the Terrace Walk to be a single storey. The cunning use of the topography demonstrates the highest engineering skill. From this elevated position, the occupants could have looked down upon the terraced gardens, or east to the 'Parc', the most likely location for coursing, hunting and other sporting pastimes. The Earl of Gainsborough carried out significant works on the East Banqueting House in the 1860s, both restoration and alterations. The changes make it more difficult to understand the original layout of the building, and now the alterations have assumed an historical significance of their own.

The West Banqueting House was subject to far less alteration than the East, and what changes there were had taken place much earlier, in the 18th century. More of the decorative plaster has survived here than in the East Banqueting House, and along with plaster from the excavations, it helps towards reconstructing the main House interiors.

There is speculation regarding the original purpose of the lower floor of the West Banqueting House. The room is large, with a handsome barrel vaulted ceiling. There are two fireplaces, although one is probably not original. The walls had once been paneled and topped with a plaster frieze. Given its size and the convenience of its location and access, this space could have been a kitchen. Thorpe's plan clearly shows a kitchen in the main House but if this was sited where it is marked on the plan, the service room would occupy a particularly favourable space so perhaps the kitchen was actually placed in the West Banqueting House. The fashionable decoration to the room does however encourage a different possibility. Perhaps this was a Banqueting House for the winter months? The Terrace level was open to the elements, and a comfortable, well heated space below would have been quite desirable. For many years this room was used as a cowshed, the gulleys in the stone floor and post holes for stalls evidence of this agricultural use. Being of a substantial size, both Banqueting Houses were rented to estate workers over the centuries.

Decorative plaster in the West Banqueting House
Landmark Trust

The lower floor of the West Banqueting House prior to restoration. The original purpose of this room is uncertain, but suggestions range from a kitchen or additional bedchamber to a winter Banqueting House or even a grotto.
Landmark Trust

The Service Court

In later centuries, the practice of siting the more functional service areas well away from the 'polite' buildings became almost ubiquitous, but in the early 17th century this fashion did not yet prevail. Servants still lived and worked almost 'cheek by jowl' with their employers and buildings tended to be relatively close together. At Campden, the service areas were hidden from the House by a series of enclosing walls. On passing through the Gatehouse and entering the Great Court, the wall on the east (left) side may have enclosed the Rose Garden and that on the west (right) concealed the Bleaching Garden with its rows of aromatic herbs. Adjacent to this stood the building known today as the Almonry.

The Almonry

Although part of the original plan and featured in the earliest bird's-eyes, the Almonry is different in style to the other buildings. It is not necessarily inferior; it does lack the architectural flourishes seen elsewhere, such as the twisting chimneys and pierced parapets, but it is an appealing example of the Cotswold vernacular style.

It is quite a small square building, standing two and a half storeys high. Its original purpose is uncertain. Identified in the Hughes Bird's-eye as the Laundry, this function is supported by its location next to the Bleaching Garden. Over the years it has been called a Hen Roost and a Pigeon House; these are probable later uses as the Almonry does stand by the Hen Yard, seen on the early bird's-eyes with its central pond. Despite these and other uses over the centuries, the internal layout is essentially unchanged, with three rooms on top of each other. The small spiral corner stair and the hearths may be slightly later additions. The basement or cellar contains a cobbled stone floor with drainage and two conduit arches in the wall which seem to be associated with the management of water. Again, this would support its use as a laundry and also perhaps a place for cold storage.

Though lacking the extravagance of the Gatehouse or Banqueting Houses, it is still a building of quality. Given that it was clearly visible above the boundary wall from Church Street, it was surely meant to form part of the approach Hicks was contriving, thus attention would have been focused on its appearance. The gables match and are axial with those on the West Banqueting House behind it. During restoration by the Landmark Trust, there was conjecture that it once had the strapwork and parapets seen on the Banqueting Houses, but this was not

The Almonry stands close to Church Street and the Almshouses, by the Hen Yard. It is clearly visible from outside the site.

conclusive. Early records refer to the *'Bleaching Garden and Garden House standing therin'* and it has been suggested that the first floor could have been an alternative Banqueting House, a space to sit away from the main house but offering a different aspect. The emphasis of the design at this site was on creating a variety of experiences; was this another?

We do not know for certain when the building was given its current name, or why. It could simply have evolved from its proximity to the Almshouses. The Almoner was charged with collecting and distributing alms, but such a role was already outdated by Hicks' time. The ground floor could have served as an estate office and

The basement or cellar contains a stone floor with drainage and two conduit arches in the wall (now filled in) which seem to be associated with the management of water. This area remains damp and sometimes wet. All this would support its use as a laundry and also perhaps a place for cold storage.

with its doors on either side on the ground floor, perhaps the needy did enter through one and exit the other having received their poor relief. However, no documentary evidence has been found to corroborate this notion.

As mentioned earlier, there was an alternative entrance at the junction of Calf Lane and Church Street. This simpler and more convenient gateway is now blocked but can be clearly seen at street level.

This 1846 engraving is a view from the Court House. It shows the drive from the alternative entrance running parallel with Church Street towards the House.
Engraving by George Hawkins from a sketch by "WM", 1846

From the High Street, Church Street leads directly to the town entrance to the site. Did Hicks build this road deliberately as part of the orchestration of the approach to his House? It would certainly have created a wonderful spectacle on turning the corner, revealing the Almshouses, the Gatehouse, the Church and the House.
National Monuments Record

The Stables

There has been much speculation about the origins of the building today known as The Court; was it the early 17th century Stables converted later into a residence by Lady Juliana, or could it even have been the original Manor House rebuilt as the Stables? If it was indeed the Stables, its location differs from that in the bird's-eyes. They don't show the building on the street corner where The Court is, but away from the road within the stable yard or courtyard. The drawings are certainly stylistically similar to The Court and the horses in the Hughes Bird's-eye are suggestive of its purpose. Presumably this is another of the discrepancies we have seen before in these images, probably drawn this way to maintain the symmetry of the picture.

The Stables were fired at the same time as the House although the extent of the damage is not known. Local legend says that Lady Juliana converted the burnt building and lived there for a time after the Civil War and study of the external elevations does support the case for a conversion. When compared with the attractiveness of the other Campden House buildings, it appears somewhat austere,

Now called The Court, it has long been supposed that this was the original Stables. The alternative entrance was immediately to the right of the building here.

Percy Rushen, the 19th century local historian, blamed the sagging to the north wall of the building on structural inadequacies dating back to its use as a stables, with its large hayloft and then the possible addition of another floor. Closer examination of the building has suggested an early timber frame. More research is needed to discover the story of this intriguing building.

even clumsy. The upper windows are small and set high under the eaves and there is a lack of symmetry not seen elsewhere. This could be attributed to a hasty conversion rather than failings in the original design. Maps indicate that this was once a larger building, but it is known to have been both extended and reduced in size over the centuries.

In the heyday of Campden House, the service area would have been a busy, bustling place. In addition to the Laundry and the Stables, there was certainly a Brewhouse, a Coach House and a Dove House, and quite possibly other buildings too. Most would have provided accommodation for whoever worked in them. The Brewhouse, as it is labelled in the Hughes Bird's-eye, appears to have been a building of some substance. It is gabled, with an entrance porch and is three stories high. It looks very grand to merely be a place to brew beer and may have also served as an estate office and accommodation. The Brewhouse no longer exists and all we know of it is what we can see in the bird's-eyes. Geophysical survey was conducted in the vicinity, but later buildings prevented clear results. The Coach House does still stand. Now a private residence, its conversion revealed large quantities of burnt stone and some medieval archaeology. There has long been conjecture that this area might be the site of the earlier Manor, but more excavation is necessary to discover if this was the case. What does seem likely are alterations to this building after the fire. An archway next to the Coach House leads directly along a causeway to the corresponding arch of Lady Juliana's Gateway, an inviting route for riding out into the countryside beyond the Gardens.

This aerial view shows the service courtyard. The Brewhouse stood between the Coach House and the Stables, under the long low building seen in the centre here. Geophysical survey revealed a distinct curve in front of The Court/Stables, some of which survives today in the form of a large flower bed. This could be the remains of the 17th century carriage turning circle.
Leonard Multon

Imagining the Pleasure Gardens

"God almighty first planted a garden and indeed it is the purest of human pleasures"

Of Gardens, 1625, Sir Francis Bacon

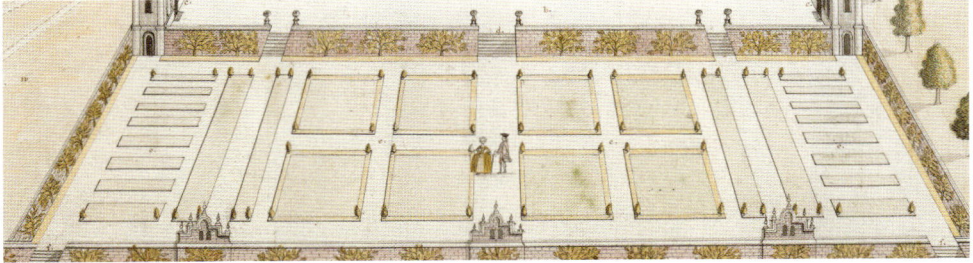

The Great Parterre: detail from the Hughes Bird's-eye, c.1750
British Library

The land to the south of Campden House ruin gives little impression today of the grand Pleasure Garden it once was, extending over 3.25 hectares (8 acres). Though we lack the detail, we can see the bare bones of the Jacobean garden layout in earthworks undisturbed since the firing of the House in 1645. As there are no contemporary records or plans for the Gardens, educated guesses have to be made as to how they may have looked. This task has been aided by aerial photography of the site together with field survey and recent archaeological and geophysical investigation (see inside back cover); and by gathering information about other early Stuart gardens. For example, Sir Francis Bacon described his ideal garden in his essay *Of Gardens* in 1625, setting out his idiosyncratic tastes and recommendations as well as giving seasonal planting advice. In the same essay he named his dislikes providing further insight into what may also have featured in our House's garden.

An open Loggia or 'garden gallery' on the south side of the House gave direct access to the gardens, forming a half-way house between inside and outside. This was a fashionable device designed to make house and garden an architectural whole. Having had to relinquish his palace and impressive gardens at Theobalds to James I, Robert Cecil, 1st Earl of Salisbury, incorporated an open loggia at his new-build at Hatfield, completed in 1611. Hicks would have been aware of this cutting edge notion given his close contact with Cecil through his brother Michael. The architectural unity of house and garden, a fundamental tenet of Jacobean garden design, marked the arrival of Italian Renaissance influences in England in the first decades of the Stuart era. With peace in Europe, travellers returned from continental trips excited by new ideas having visited sophisticated Renaissance gardens in Italy – the Villa d'Este, with its descending terraces was especially admired.

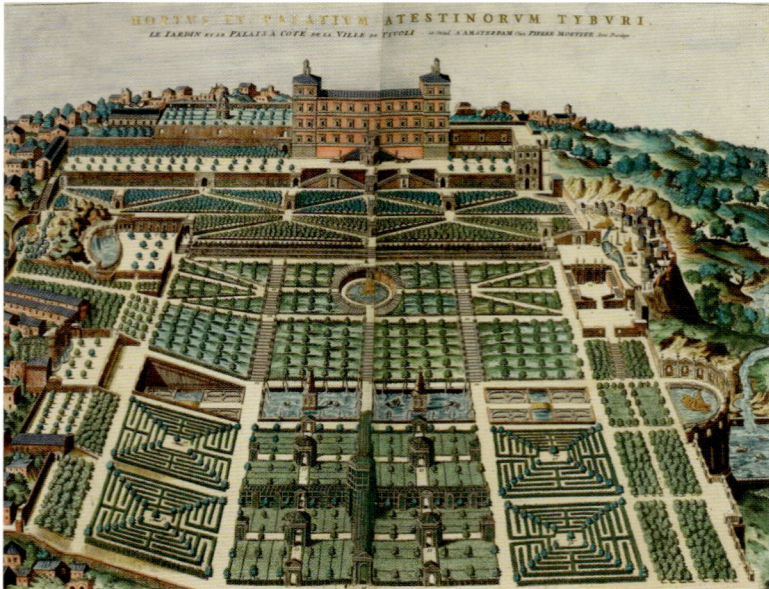

Bird's-eye of the gardens at Villa d'Este, bet. 1560-75, Étienne Dupérac

In the first decade of James' reign, a number of grand Jacobean gardens based on Renaissance ideas of symmetry were created; Campden's garden was one of these. It represented a short transition between the earlier Tudor garden and the classical arcadian garden which followed the early Stuart period. The Queen and Prince Henry, her eldest son and heir to the throne, employed leading continental designers and led the field with innovative gardens at Somerset House and Richmond Palace. They established fashions in garden style followed by wealthy men rising through the social ranks, eager to secure their place in Society. Hicks was just such a man.

Creating the Gardens

It is immediately evident that the land to the south below Campden House has been greatly reconfigured. Hicks sited his mansion on high ground with the church forming an impressive backdrop. Many man-hours must have been spent on massive earth moving endeavours, taking advantage of the natural topography to sculpt the sloping land below the House to form terraced gardens in the Italianate style. While the East Banqueting House was being renovated by the Landmark Trust in 1990 an archaeological excavation recorded that many metres of made up ground formed the platform on which the house would be built.

We do not know who designed the gardens but they appear to have been created as a complete symmetrical scheme integral with the position of the House and are essentially early Stuart in concept with vistas or prospects as pleasures to be enjoyed.

The Terrace Walk

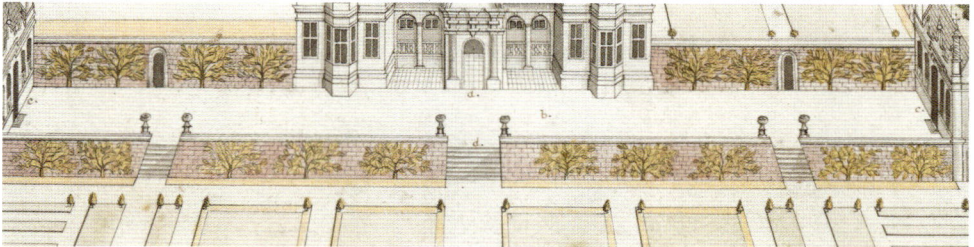

Steps, walls and espaliered trees: detail from the Hughes Bird's-eye, c.1750
British Library

On leaving Hicks' mansion via the Loggia, one would have emerged onto the Terrace Walk leading to Banqueting Houses at either end, possibly bordered on the south side by a stone balustrade. Wooden balustrading was used at Hatfield but with a plentiful supply of local stone we may be certain that stone was the material of choice throughout the gardens at Campden. The Terrace Walk, wide enough for visitors to stroll several abreast, probably had a well-constructed hard surface and was not grassed as it is now. Below the balustrade were steeply descending formal gardens with views stretching over the water meadows between the Scuttlebrook and River Cam to the countryside beyond. It is quite possible that Hicks enclosed adjacent land to enhance the setting of his new house and gardens as well giving the impression of a surrounding private parc.

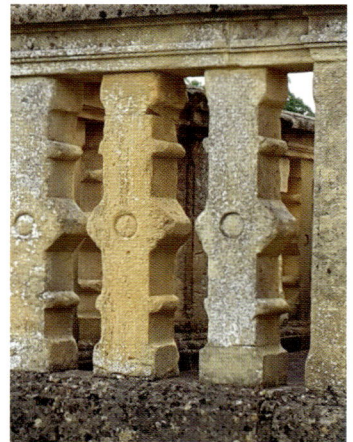

Balustrading to the East Banqueting House, possibly original
CCHS

The Terrace Walk balustrade, possibly embellished with urns of gillyflowers and statuary, was breached in the middle and at both ends by flights of stone steps descending to the Great Parterre some three metres below.

The Great Parterre

The Grand Parterre was a large level garden in the Renaissance tradition measuring over sixty metres square. Today this is a rough square of grass bordered on three sides by high, steeply sloping banks; however archaeological excavation has revealed that originally stone walling would have held back the earth. Over the centuries the stone has no doubt been robbed out with consequent earth slippage. Archaeological drawings and photographs from the excavation undertaken in 1990 recorded part of a retaining wall some four metres high at the north east corner.

The Great Parterre gave the impression of a sunken garden surrounded by high walls reminiscent of a Tudor privy garden: an enclosed private garden to be enjoyed whilst walking within or viewed from terraces above. The practice of training fruit trees against walls leaving a bed of earth in front to provide nourishment for the roots was established by the early 17th century. William Lawson emphasises the importance of allowing room for tree roots to grow in *A New Orchard and Garden, 1618 "…to plant apricots, cherries and peaches…. and flatten them to a wall ..is …hurtful .. for the wall hinders the roots"*. The geophysical survey shows a high resistance linear feature suggesting that a path ran round the perimeter of the Great Parterre a few metres out from the garden walls. High walls, a structural necessity at Campden, offered protection against wind and trapped the heat of the sun. Espaliered fruit trees, decorative and productive, displayed the wealth of an owner with the means to employ a team of skilled gardeners.

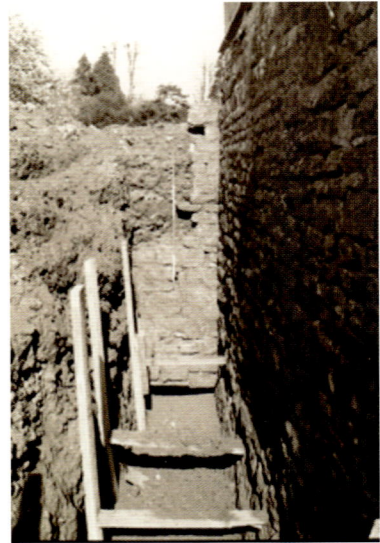

Excavation revealed remnants of the retaining wall, built to support the Terrace Walk and House platform. It was obviously a very substantial structure, measuring some 4 metres high. This view looks north towards the Churchyard, with the west wall of the East Banqueting House to the right.
© Gloucestershire County Council Archaeology Service

"the fittest time of the moone for proyning, is, as of grafting, when the sap is ready to stire"

Quotation and image from A New Orchard and Garden, 1618, William Lawson

All the bird's-eye views show three decorative gabled stone pavilions protruding from the southern wall providing seated viewing and overlooking the lower terraces. Geophysics supports the drawings in this respect, recording three distinct areas of high resistance, one at each end and the other in the middle of the wall although any possible extant foundations were overlaid by Civil War defences identified in the archaeological excavation.

Pavilion: detail from the Hughes Bird's-eye, c.1750
British Library

The Great Parterre was divided into compartments by wide paths in the form of the 'Union Flag' (established by Royal Proclamation 1606): could this have been another statement of Hicks' loyalty to King James? Conversely, the diagonal paths may simply be a happy coincidence, providing immediate access from the three flights of steps on the north side depicted in all the bird's-eye drawings and appearing as areas of high resistance in the geophysical survey. The layouts of paths shown in aerial photographs and confirmed by geophysics demonstrate that the later bird's-eye views of the Parterre layout were inaccurate; though the earliest does show a pair of Parterre gardens of similar design. John Parkinson, the plantsman, recommended that *'allies'* (paths) be spacious to preserve valuable plants from harm in *Paradisi in Sole* published in 1629.

Archaeological excavation revealed that they were wide and exceptionally well-constructed with a concave base of large stones filled with successively smaller stones and topped with finely crushed stone: Hicks spared no expense in the building of his gardens.

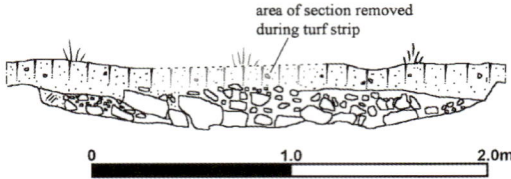

Archaeological section drawing of path construction; 'a' on the photograph
CCHS excavation, 2014

Digging the paths on the Great Parterre
b – stone path, c – earth beds
CCHS excavation, 2014

At the intersection of these paths, geophysics recorded a high resistance area several metres in diameter suggesting a large paved area at the centre of the Great Parterre. Although the geophysical readings had suggested a fully paved central area, excavation revealed, unexpectedly, that in the middle there was circular stone lined void filled with earth free of stones, with clay at its base: it is possible that the earth could have been a later in-fill. Further excavation found that the area surrounding the void was made up of a thick layer of clay laid down during construction with substantial stones placed over it. A covering of smaller stones made a relatively flat surface. Clearly this was a foundation built to support something of a very great weight.

The interpretation of this feature is uncertain. One would expect a prominent statement in such a central position in the Great Parterre and some have suggested a statue or sundial; more probable is a stone water basin above the ground, incorporating an ornamental fountain with a central cistern set into the ground beneath. It is possible that there could have

Stone lined void with clay base
at the centre of the Great Parterre
CCHS excavation, 2018

been combination of all three features. The central void had a channel cut through the clay base leading in a north-westerly direction, though no pipe work was discovered. An elaborate fountain at Trinity College, Cambridge, commissioned slightly earlier in 1601, incorporated a lead cistern at its base which served as a source of water as well as being decorative; could the gardeners at Campden have found a water-filled basin at the foot of a fountain useful as a dipping pond for filling their watering buckets in the summer months?

"Fountains they are a great beauty and refreshment"
Of Gardens, *1625*,
Francis Bacon

The fountain and pool in the Privy Garden at Hatfield give an impression of how the centre of The Great Parterre could have looked. 2017

Sophisticated fountains and hydraulic automata were fashionable in Jacobean gardens. Salomon de Caus, a French Huguenot hydraulic engineer and polymath working for the Stuart Court (and Robert Cecil at Hatfield), was hugely influential and inventive; he published a record of his many English projects in *Les Raisons des Forces Mouvantes* in 1615. The spring water piped down from the Conduit House high above Chipping Campden would have provided an adequate head of water to support an impressive fountain; surely a 'must have' in Hicks' Pleasure Gardens. The two earliest bird's-eye views show a central circular feature which may depict a pool or fountain.

Whereas there is reasonable certainty about the hard landscaping features of a Jacobean Parterre, the soft landscaping is more problematic. At Campden we know the pattern of paths produced eight triangular compartments of earth but there is no indication as to how these would have appeared. A soil analysis was unhelpful.

Some gardeners deployed coloured sands and gravels to produce decorative symmetrical patterns though Francis Bacon disapproved of any such quick fix solutions: *"as for making knots with divers coloured earths .. you may see as good sights ..in tarts"*! It seems more likely that Pleasure Gardens such as Campden's would have employed sophisticated planting schemes which may have varied from year to year as fashions changed. Many styles ran concurrently from the late Tudor period to the Civil War. The Elizabethan knot garden was planted with medicinal herbs and scented flowers; through the Stuart period increasingly intricate designs were adopted, culminating in the elaborate French 'broderie' style of interlaced curving patterns of planting.

Gervase Markham, garden pamphleteer, remarked "now [knots] only popular with the vulgar" in 1613

Knot Garden designs from The Country Housewife's Garden, 1618, William Lawson

Alternatively, beds could be laid with carefully selected turf either left as simple grass compartments or cut into patterns. Thomas Hill gives instructions for laying out knot patterns in *The Gardener's Labrinthe* first published in 1590 and a garden account book at Chatsworth lists *"a dozenne of packs of threads for lynes"* for marking out the designs. The English love affair with grass was born. This was no easy option requiring constant maintenance involving frequent scything and beating down to a level surface with heavy stone or wooden rollers. A 1609 account from Hatfield talks of *"making an end of laying all the grass plats"* and *"laying grass quarters"*. This close mown turf was considered sophisticated and favoured by Francis Bacon: *"nothing is more pleasant to the eye than green grass kept finely shorn"*. Clipped cypress obelisks and evergreen topiary added vertical accents and pots of rare specimens might also have been displayed here to add interest.

Some early 17th century garden pamphlets

The Country Housewife's Garden, *1618,*
William Lawson;
A new Orchard and Garden, *1618,*
William Lawson;
The English Husbandman, *1613,*
Gervase Markham;
The Gardener's Labyrinth, *1594,*
Thomas Hill
Glasgow University

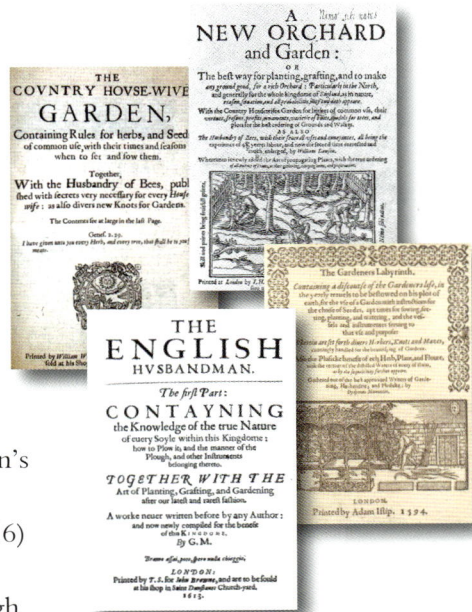

Design ideas were circulated in pamphlets with woodcut illustrations. William Lawson's *The Country Housewife's Garden* (1618) and Gervase Markham's *The Country Farm* (1616) included knot garden designs and gave English specific cultivation advice. Although aimed primarily at the wealthy gentry class, they reached wider sectors of society and several had dedications to aristocratic patrons. In 1610, John Gerard presented his *Herbal: the Historie of Plants* with specially coloured plates to The Bodleian Library and Gervase Markham's books are listed in the library inventories of William Cavendish, Earl of Devonshire and Robert Cecil. Henry Percy, 9th Earl of Northumberland, even took a copy of the 1608 edition of Thomas Hill's *A Gardener's Labyrinth* into the Tower of London with him.

This was the era of plant collecting. In 1610, Robert Cecil sent his gardener, John Tradescant, to Europe to source exotic new plants coming into the Low Countries from Turkey, the Levant and the New World for his garden at Hatfield. Though there was intense rivalry between the owners of grand gardens, treasured plants were given as presents or sometimes exchanged. Hicks probably had early news of exciting new introductions with his Hatfield contacts or, as a leading mercer trading

Gervase Markham says of the Crown Imperial "of all the flowers both forraigne and home bred, the delicatest and strangest; it has the true shape of an Emeriall crown"

Image from **Hortus Floridus**, *1614, Crispin van der Pass*

through the Low Countries, he may have been importing direct. Crown Imperials, Auriculas and Tulips became immensely popular. The plantsman John Parkinson observes *"the crown imperial for his stately beautifulness deserveth the first place in this our garden of delight"*.

"... boxe is best, and it was set thicke, at least eighteene inches broad at the bottome & being kept with clipping."
Gervase Markham in The English Husbandman, 1613

Image from **Florilegium, 1612, Emanuel Sweert**

Introduced to a *"small, dwarf kinde* [of shrub] *called French or Dutch Box"* by the Flemish gardening community in London and taught how to manage it, John Parkinson favoured it as an edging plant to protect beds of rare specimen plants and, though previously unpopular with Elizabethans because of its unpleasant smell, its use became popular even though there was *"a want of a good sweet scent"*.

Intended as a sales catalogue with plants listed by seasons of the year this frontispiece perfectly encapsulates formal Jacobean style showing ornate balustrading with steps leading down to a formal parterre garden with paths between knots sparsely planted with prized newly introduced crown imperials, tulips and hyacinths edged with box; topiary provides higher accents within the beds. The garden is enclosed with plant covered arbours.
Frontispiece to the Spring Garden from **Hortus Floridus, 1614, Crispin de Passe**

Estate archives, library inventories, garden pamphlets and sales catalogues are sources of information about plants being used at the time. Hicks was a benefactor of John Tradescant's 'Ark', a collection of curiosities. Tradescant produced a list of collected items together with a catalogue of plants available for sale at his Lambeth nursery garden. The planting of these rarities would appear sparse to the modern eye as they were displayed as botanical specimens to be admired individually for their aesthetic qualities. Non-hardy plants may have been grown in pots and taken indoors in unseasonable weather or when guests were not visiting the garden.

Detail from **The Capel Family, c1640, Cornelius Johnson** ©National Portrait Gallery

The background view shows the parterre garden at Hadham established in the 1630s, a sophisticated formal layout with many embellishments fashionable under Charles I. Lady Capel (shown in the portrait) was a granddaughter of Hicks and one may assume she was familiar with the Jacobean Pleasure Gardens at Campden and therefore took a particular interest in the gardens at Hadham. Roy Strong pointed out that valuable garden design information can be gleaned from the background views in portraits of this time. See also the Hampden portrait, page 17.

Side Terraces and Tunnel Arbours

To the east and west above the Great Parterre were two raised side terraces. Francis Bacon suggests that their surfaces should *"ever be finely gravelled, and no grass because of going wet"* and the geophysical survey confirmed that Campden's Side Terraces were hard surfaced. They could have been open walks to match the Terrace Walk in front of the House, but more likely they would have been topped with another fashionable feature: Tunnel Arbours similar to those in the 'Spring Garden' *Hortus Floridus* (see facing page). No archaeological work has yet been carried out to verify this. A foreign visitor to Thomas Cecil's Wimbledon in 1618 admires his *"covered walks…and lofty hedges"*.

Tunnel Arbours accentuated the sunken aspect of the Great Parterre below. They would have been formed of bent willow poles or constructed of elaborate carpentry work, providing walkways shaded from the sun and sheltered from the wind. Windows from which to admire the Great Parterre below and view the outer reaches of the garden might also have been incorporated into the woven branches. Thomas Hill suggests covering the arches with cucumber, melon and grapevines and, for fragrance, jasmine, honeysuckle and climbing roses in *A Gardener's Labyrinth*. Plants would be secured with osiers ties; and sally gardens (osier beds) are known to have existed close to the gardens at Campden. Tunnel Arbours might also have been made by pleaching trees.

John Aubrey, the 17th century diarist, recalled that Bacon hung coloured and gilded glass in his 'hedges' to catch the light and delight the onlooker, mirroring the reflection of the sunlight playing on the huge expanses of window glass in his Gorhambury house.

Pleached trees at Ham House, 2018

"...this hedge...set all with flowers"
Of Gardens, *1625, Francis Bacon*

Musk rose and clematis from **Hortus Floridus**, *1614,*
Crispin de Passe

"…to plant a covert alle. by which you may go in the shade"
Of Gardens, *1625, Francis Bacon*

A Gardener's Labyrinth, *1594,*
Thomas Hill
Glasgow University

Francis Bacon observed "that when the wind blows sharp, you may walk [in a tunnel arbour] *as in a gallery"*

Long Gallery at Chastleton House
Steve Gledhill/VirtuallyGrey

Paula Henderson suggests that walking in the long gallery indoors at Chastleton with its intricate, plant inspired domed plaster work ceiling would have brought to mind the pleasures of strolling through a flower covered arbour in a garden.

There are two terraces below the East Side Terrace. Could the lower of the two have been a bowling green entered from the south door of the East Banqueting House? Bowling was a universally popular sport at the time and the geophysics clearly indicates that this terrace was not paved as no areas of high resistance show up here to suggest a hard surface. Prince Henry had a bowling green built at St. James' Park in 1610 and Sir Thomas Tresham planned to have one at Lyveden New Bield. Hicks' brother Michael had a bowling alley at Ruckholt, his house in Essex, and from correspondence between the two, we know that both brothers played bowls. In 1604 Sir Robert Wrothe writes to Michael inviting him to play bowls and eat oysters, reminding him to bring Baptist with him. Campden House and its Pleasure Gardens were built for recreation and entertainment and as the middle terrace too appears to have had an unpaved area; could there have been butts for archery here? William Lawson writing in 1618 recommends *"a pair of archery butts to stretch your arms".*

William Lawson suggests that in an ideal garden "it shall be a pleasure to have a bowling green" in **A New Orchard and Garden,** *1618*

Bowling, 16th century woodcut

The Great Orchard

Walking southwards down steps from the Great Parterre, we reach a series of shallow descending terraces probably formed by low retaining walls; this was the Great Orchard which extends further to east and west than the Great Parterre above. A few gnarled fruit trees remain there today. The original planting would have been of prized young specimens, arranged in orderly fashion to be admired for pleasure not merely valued for their produce. John Tradescant was sent to the Low Countries by Robert Cecil to buy trees for his orchard at Hatfield; bills from Holland included varieties of medlar, quince, mulberry, pear, cherry and apple. Cecil also received gifts for his garden; five hundred fruit trees from the French Queen and fifty orchard trees from Sir Thomas Tresham's widow. Recent research by the National Trust has revealed some three hundred planting pits at Tresham's orchards at Lyveden New Bield. No doubt Hicks would have been keen to establish one at Campden too.

Robert Cecil sent his gardener, Mountain Jennings, to view the orchard at Lyveden New Bield " ... to pick some such observations as may enable him to spend my money to better purpose" describing it as "one of the fairest orchards that is in England"

A New Orchard and Garden, *1618, William Lawson*

The Water Gardens

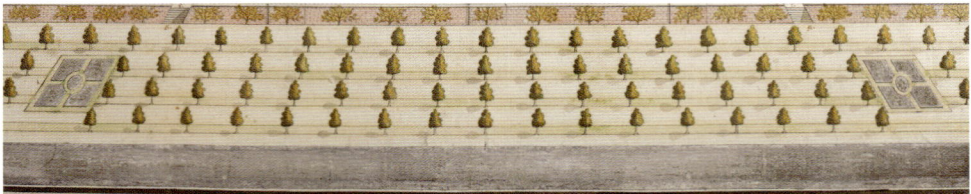

The Water Gardens: detail from Hughes Bird's-eye, c1750
British Library

Perhaps the ultimate delights to be found Campden's Pleasure Gardens were in the Water Gardens, so much favoured in the grandest of early 17th century estates. In 1611 Robert Cecil was creating The Dell, a complex of canals and water features at Hatfield whilst, at the same time, Prince Henry planned extravagant water gardens at Richmond. Sir Walter Cope, Hicks' Kensington neighbour at Cope Castle (later

Holland House), built extensive water gardens and was also intimately involved in planning the work at Hatfield. Sir Anthony Cope, another family member, embarked on an even more ambitious scheme at Hanwell Castle. Campden had advantages over many early Stuart gardens as the land forming the gardens sloped down to streams readily adaptable to the needs of such a project. Hicks was rich enough to afford the enormous costs of construction, for this was taming nature on a grand scale involving huge feats of engineering.

The Ornamental Canal

Below the Great Orchard at Campden ran an artificial Canal running west to east and forming the southern boundary of the Pleasure Gardens. This was not a meandering river but a straight strip of water probably deep enough for boating, some three hundred metres long with short right-angled turns at each end. A 1722 Estate Map shows the Canal and the two terminals, now named Fletchers Boat Pool.

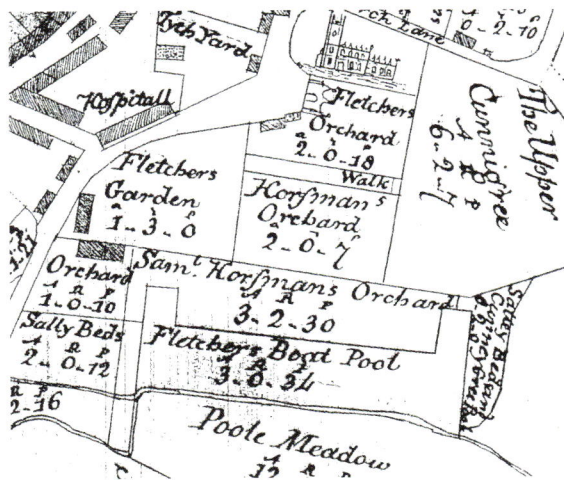

Detail from 1722 Estate Map showing Fletchers Boat Pool with the two terminals
Leicestershire, Leicester & Rutland Record Office, courtesy of the Exton Estate

Canal and bank at Lyveden New Bield, 2018

The site of the Canal is still clearly discernible as a water-logged area, thickly overgrown with bulrushes and reeds. The Scuttlebrook that runs nearby would have been used as a constant source of water whereas Sir Thomas Tresham had to rely on rain water to fill the canals at Lyveden New Bield. Banks on either side of the Canal served as raised walks which, one may imagine, would be planted with trees and scented shrubs and under-planted with violets, primroses and strawberries.

"I know a bank where the wild thyme blows, Where oxslips and the nodding violet grows, Quite over-canopied with luscious woodbine, With sweet musk-rose and with eglantine"
A Midsummer Night's Dream, *Shakespeare*

Illustrations from **Gerard's Herbal: the history of plants,** *1597, John Gerard*

Violet   Musk rose and eglantine

The banks were intended to be enjoyed whilst boating or strolling along; they also afforded views across the water and up to the Great Orchard with glimpses of the House above introducing yet another carefully orchestrated Renaissance garden experience. The Canal would be stocked with fish and ornamental birds providing angling and water fowling in addition to boating as leisure activities.

Bacon particularly recommended three plants "to have the pleasure when you walk or tread" and "which perfume the air most delightfully…being trodden upon and crushed: burnet, wilde thyme and watermints." Of Gardens, 1625, Francis Bacon.

Illustrations from **Gerard's Herbal: the history of plants,** *1597, John Gerard*

Burnet   Thyme   Watermint

The Water Parterre

Known recently as 'the newt pond' by local lads, the overgrown square of five water filled compartments at the eastern end of the Canal was originally a Water Parterre forming part of the sophisticated Water Gardens at Campden. Not visible from the House or the Great Parterre, it had an element of a delightful surprise. The compartments are still full of water and, though overgrown, the basic plan is clearly visible. Reached on foot or on disembarking from a boat, Campden's Water Parterre was geometric with four corner chambers surrounding a central pool separated by walkways. This is clearly shown in the William Hughes drawing and recorded in the field survey too. The walls and floors of the compartments of water could have been lined with coloured glass and lustrous pebbles giving the effect of a glittering jewel.

Detail of aerial photograph showing the remains of the Water Parterre

John Aubrey, writing later in the 17th century, recalls that at Gorhambury, Francis Bacon's *"ponds were filled with clear water, through which coloured pebbles arranged in the shape of fishes etc could be seen…and if a poor person brought his lordship half a dozen pebbles of curious shape he would give them a shilling"*. Hatfield account books record that John Tradescant imported *"…eyght boxes of shells"* to decorate Robert Cecil's Water Gardens. Fountains are a possibility. Stone balustrading might have enclosed this formal feature and there are indications on the geophysical readings that there was a paved surround.

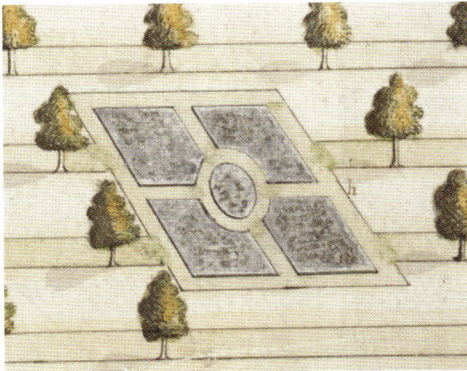

" ..some fine pavement about it" and *"..encompassed also with fine rails"*
Of Gardens, 1625, Francis Bacon

The five chambered water parterre: detail from the Hughes Bird's-eye, c.1750
British Library

The William Hughes drawing shows a matching Water Parterre at the west end of the Canal and there are signs on the ground and in the geophysical survey that this may have been the case: certainly Renaissance rules of symmetry in garden design would suggest this. If so, it appears that the later construction of a causeway leading from the stables to Lady Juliana's Gateway may have interfered with a west Water Parterre. Opinions are divided on the matter.

The Prospect Mount

The final Jacobean garden feature still discernible today is a Prospect Mount, now much reduced from its original height. The Mount is situated in the southwest corner of the field called The Coneygree just outside the perimeter of the Pleasure Gardens. Possibly constructed from canal spoil, the Mount afforded views or prospects back to the House across the Great Orchard and to the Water Parterre glittering just below, as well as drawing attention to the extent of Hicks' landholdings. Reached through an opening in a boundary wall which shows clearly on the geophysics, a visit to the Mount would be an adventure into the land beyond the garden for more al fresco pleasures; it also formed an elevated observation platform to view coursing or falconry on The Coneygree provided for the entertainment of guests. Francis Bacon would *"have a mount of some pretty height .. to look abroad into the fields"*. Access to the summit was by paths, possibly spiralling like Lyveden New Bield's snail mounts or by means of steps.

The background of this portrait is said to be Coombe Abbey where Princess Elizabeth resided when the ward of John Harington of Exton. The Exton estate was later acquired by Hicks and became the principal seat of the family.

In the background to the left we see a winding path ascending to a Prospect Mount with an elaborate Arbour at the top and on the right an arched bridge over a Canal leading to a boundary palisade dividing the landscape gardens from the parc beyond. Princess Elizabeth, daughter of James I, 1603, Robert Peake.
National Maritime Museum

John Evelyn, in his **Elysium Britannicum,** *suggests that viewing mounts are best situated towards "the remoter part" … "as from where to take a universal prospect not only of the garden but the whole country"*

One of the snail mounts at Lyveden New Bield, 2018

The RCHME field survey records a feature which could be a second Mount situated in outlying countryside to the south beyond the water meadows by the Cam.

Household Gardens

Subsequent leases of the land at Campden refer to a Rose Garden to the east of the House and, in support, the bird's-eye drawings do show flower beds to the east, though there is no evidence of them on the ground. The Household Gardens at Campden House would probably have been in the service area to the west of the House, separated from the Pleasure Gardens: the strips of long narrow beds shown in the Hughes watercolour may represent the Bleaching Gardens near to the Laundry where linen was draped over aromatic bushes to dry and whiten in the sun. Herbs and vegetables for the household might also have been grown here.

Possible Bleaching Garden: detail from the Hughes Bird's-eye, c.1750
British Library

The Great Sink

On the south western perimeter of the Pleasure Gardens lies the area known as the Great Sink where the Scuttlebrook enters the site. This is a low lying wet area, west of a causeway of uncertain date connecting the Stables (now The Court) and Lady Juliana's Gateway. Lady Juliana's Gateway probably post-dates the formal Jacobean gardens and may have been a Caroline (Charles I) addition giving an access to the wider countryside. The fact that the Gateway is named after Lady Juliana, Hicks' daughter, does suggest that it could have been built by her after his death. An elongated pool to the north may be the *'Stew Pond'* (fish pond) mentioned in one lease. The intriguing square of land surrounded by ditches has been variously interpreted as a "mediaeval moated manor house", "a lake" or "a Caroline Water Garden incorporating a water spiral walk or labyrinth". Clearly further research is needed here.

View south through the archway from the Service Court along the causeway towards Lady Juliana's Gateway

Lady Juliana's Gateway
CCHS

Detail of the decoration on the south side of Lady Julian's Gateway; perhaps marking the entrance to the private Pleasure Gardens

In summary, using clues from a variety of sources and backed up with recent geophysical and archaeological excavation, we have attempted to re-create a convincing picture of the grandeur of the magnificent Pleasure Gardens at Campden. The site represents the remains of one of very few undisturbed Jacobean gardens and as such it is of particular interest and importance. William Lawson presented a distillation of the essentials of a Jacobean garden in a helpful diagram in *A New Orchard and Garden*, 1618. It appears from this illustration that Hicks incorporated all these salient features.

William Lawson's essential features in a Jacobean Garden from **A New Orchard and Garden, 1618.**

KEY
A trees/ornaments – topiary
B formal orchard
C knots – parterre garden
D kitchen garden
F conduits – fountains
G varying levels with steps – terracing
H walks – covered arbours
I 'wilderness' walks – orchard walks
K boundary 'fencing' – walls/trellises
M prospect mounts
P water – canal/river/pools; water gardens

The diagram also specifies E bridges, L 'outer fence', N still-house and O standing for bees.

"*So I have made a platform of a princely garden…*
and in this I have spared no cost"
Of Gardens, 1625, Francis Bacon

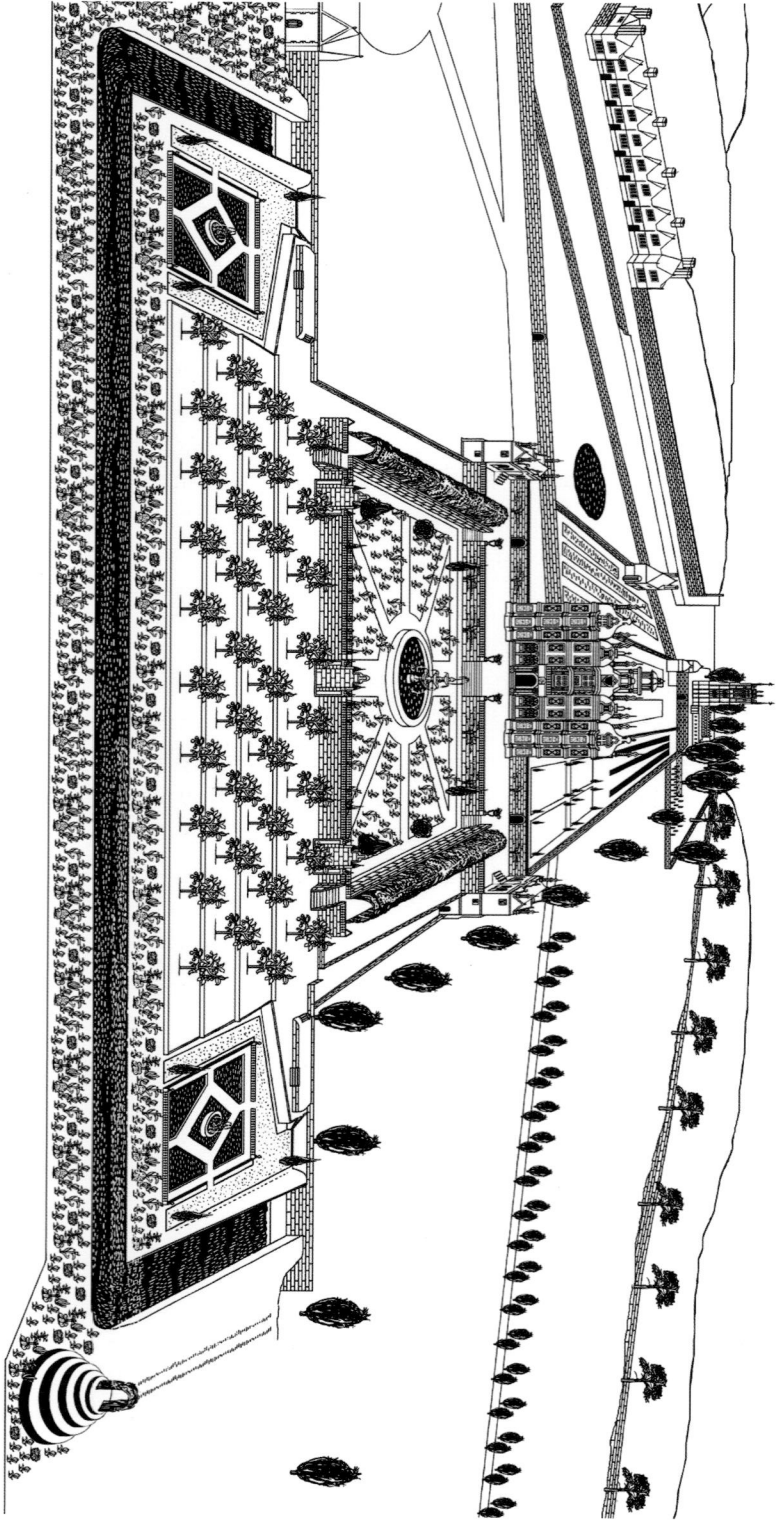

The CCHS Bird's-Eye, 2018

This new image, made in the style of the earlier bird's-eyes, illustrates how we think the House and Gardens may have looked, based on the results of all our research.

Tom Ford, 2018

"The Great Burnt Manor House"

(From a lease in the Exton Papers, 1691)

Hicks died in 1629. His funeral must have been a momentous event in Chipping Campden. In the Church there is a magnificent memorial tomb to the town's most important benefactor. His will does not specify who now owned the House, however the contents were left to his daughter, Juliana, and local legend says she lived there. Some of the stylistic differences in the design suggest that work continued into the mid 17th century. Had Hicks given Juliana the property before his death? Or perhaps his widow, Elizabeth, retained ownership but had no interest in being resident? On Elizabeth's death in 1643 the House was definitely passed to Juliana and her husband, Edward Noel. But by this time, Civil War was tearing the country apart, and when it came to Chipping Campden, its impact was terrible and the destruction devastating.

The town's location was of strategic importance as it was near the crossing point of two major military routes: one used by the Parliamentarians from Gloucester up to Warwick and the other by the Royalists from Worcester across to Oxford. Troops were moving rapidly from place to place and Campden was held at times by both Royalists and Parliamentarians. In 1644 Prince Rupert ordered the House to be occupied and fortified. Colonel William Legge wrote to the Prince on Christmas Day 1644, confirming his arrival and saying that he feared *'a famine rather than the enemy'*, such was the scarcity of supplies to be found. Like hundreds of other places during the War, a

Woodcut from a pamphlet **The Cruel Practices of Prince Rupert,** *1643*

combination of garrisoned troops and raiding parties had decimated the town of its men, its food and its supplies. A ruthless new commander was appointed, Colonel Henry Bard, taking residence with his officers in Hicks' beautiful House and billeting the soldiers in the town. He wrote to the Prince in early 1645, *"May it please your Highnesse Excellency, I thought good to signify to you that I am here at Cambden House, with my forces, which I conceive will be very advantageous … we are taking great pains with spades, mattocks and shovels …"*.

During the excavation of the Great Parterre, the first evidence of this building of fortifications referred to by Bard is thought to have been discovered. The path running along the southern perimeter of the Parterre was found to be overlaid by a bank of earth and stone. It clearly postdates the early 17th century path and no evidence was found to suggest it was of a much later date. We know that no substantial changes were made to the site in later centuries and so archaeologists have interpreted it as the remains of ramparts constructed during the Civil War. It would be an obvious place to build defensive earthworks, offering a panoramic view of the surrounding countryside. These fortifications were probably incomplete and the effort abandoned when the occupying forces left.

In May 1645, King Charles led his army out of Oxford and westwards. As they marched, they gathered troops from their garrisons along the way. There are varying accounts of who gave the order to set fire to Campden House but it was common practice to destroy such bases to prevent the enemy making use of them. Sir Henry Slingsby says in his Memoirs, Prince Rupert *'commanded it to be burnt, which I set on a light fire before we marched off; a house as my Lord Cambden says hath cost £33,000; in building and in furniture.'* A London news sheet, *Weekly Account*, reported on 12 May 1645 *'On Saturday last his Majesty in the evening went down by Broadway to Evesham; and Prince Rupert marched in the rearguard over Broadway hill by the light of Cambden House which they say was then on fire'*. Regardless of who gave the order, the House was deliberately set alight; the ensuing blaze was visible for miles around.

After its destruction, building material from the House was used locally and you can still spot pieces of the distinctive burnt pink limestone around the town today. Given the dearth of finds from the excavations, it is probable that the clearing of the site was conducted quite systematically. The notion of locals taking stone whenever they needed it is a popular one, but this was a private property owned by the Lord of the Manor and the bulk of the remains may have been removed in a methodical manner. The site stayed in the ownership of the Noel family until the end of the 20th century, when it was handed over to the care of the Landmark Trust.

One final curiosity is the remaining stump of the House. Nothing has been left of any value or use except one fragment of wall. Perhaps it was preserved as a memorial to Hicks and his Royalist family who sacrificed much during the Civil War. It is certainly a permanent reminder of this beautiful Jacobean House.

"Friday May 9. His Majestie marched to Evesham … in the primeir place was Prince Rupert's regiment … This day … 300 foot taken out of our garrison of Camden; the howse which was so Faire burnt."

Diary of the Marches of the Royal Army During the Great Civil War
by Captain Richard Symonds, 1644-6

Suggested reading

Ingenious Endeavours: The Life of Baptist Hicks

A Cotswold Family by Susan Hicks Beach

Servant of the Cecils by Alan G. R. Smith

Elizabeth's London by Liza Picard

The Time Traveller's Guide to Elizabethan England by Ian Mortimer

History of Parliament Online: www.historyofparliamentonline.org

Middlesex County Records: Volume 4: 1667-88 pp 329-349, Sir Baptist Hicks : www.british-history.ac.uk

The Theater of His Hospitality: The Buildings of Campden House

The Tudor and Jacobean Country House, A Building History by Malcolm Airs

Houses of the Gentry 1480-1680 by Nicholas Cooper

The Jacobean Country House by Nicholas Cooper

The World of the Country House in Seventeenth Century England by J.T. Cliffe

Elizabethan Architecture by Mark Girouard

Elizabethan and Jacobean Style by Timothy Mowl

Imagining the Pleasure Gardens

The Tudor House and Garden by Paula Henderson

The Artist and the Garden by Roy Strong

The Renaissance Garden in England by Roy Strong

Strange Blooms: The Curious Lives and Adventures of the John Tradescants by Jennifer Potter

The Making of the English Gardener: Plants, Books and Inspiration 1560 – 1660 by Margaret Willes

General Campden History

Campden: A New History by Members of CADHAS

I Marched Straight to Cambden by Jill Wilson

Old Campden House by Caroline Stanford

More research papers about Campden House by members of the Society and other useful resources can be found on the CCHS website in the Campden House Archive.

Details from the CCHS Geophysical Resistance Surveys (2014 and 2018), The Field Survey (RCHME 1984) and the Aerial Photograph of the Campden Site (NMR 23321/06/2003) highlighting features in the pleasure gardens

The geophysical surveys undertaken by CCHS under the supervision of Archeoscan took the form of Electrical Resistance Surveys (sometimes referred to as Resistivity Surveys). Buried stone structures such as walls or paths are generally poor electrical conductors compared to the surrounding soils which usually have higher moisture content. When an electrical current is passed through the ground, stone features show up as *high resistance*, **seen as white on the geophysical survey images below**. Black line squares are the 20m survey grids.

The location of the three CCHS Resistance Surveys illustrated on this page:
1. The Great Parterre
2. The East Side Terraces
3. The Water Parterre

1. The Great Parterre Resistance Survey
CCHS 2014 with interpretative key:
a) stone steps   e) central feature
b) perimeter path   f) triangular 'flower
c) pavilions   beds'
d) paths

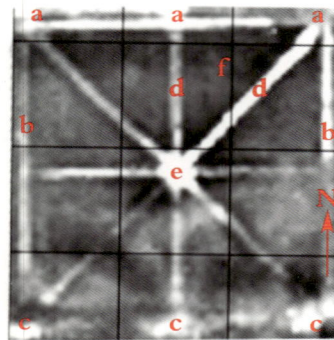

2. The East Side Terraces Resistance Survey CCHS 2018

3. The East Water Parterre Resistance Survey CCHS 2018

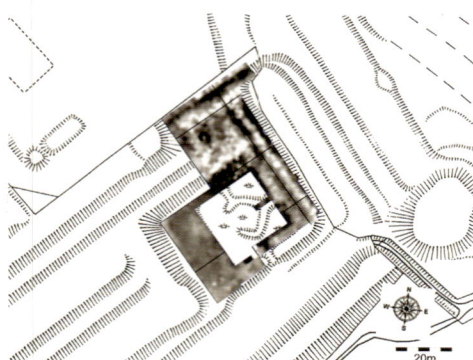

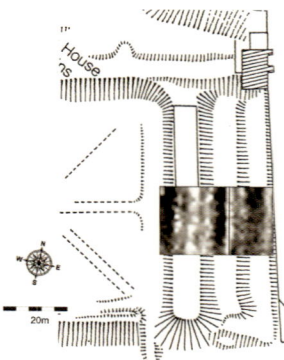

This survey indicates that some of the terracing was paved. This is particularly clear on the upper terrace.

These readings suggest that walls and paving surrounded the Water Parterre.